STEP ONE: THE GOSPEL AND THE GHETTO

By Harv Oostdyk

A Prestige Book
Published By
SONLIFE INTERNATIONAL

STEP ONE: THE GOSPEL AND THE GHETTO
Copyright 1983 by Harv Oostdyk
All rights reserved. No part of this
book may be reproduced or transmitted
in any form or by any means, electronic
or mechanical, including photocopying, recording
or by any information storage and retrieval
system, without permission in writing from the
publisher. SonLife International Inc. Box 354,
Basking Ridge, N.J. 07920.
Printed in the United States of America
International Standard Book Number 089-221-094-X

Distributed by New Leaf Press
Harrison, Arkansas 72601

This book is dedicated to Clint W. Murchison, Jr.
who in unusual ways gave his leadership
and concern to help the poor.

*". . . The godly man gives generously to the poor.
His good deeds will be an honor to him forever."*
II Cor. 9:9

ACKNOWLEDGMENT

I wish to extend appreciation to Debbie Boyce, Bill Boyce, Billie Cunningham, Jeff Fendley, Maureen Hornstein, Sam Kohl, Randy Matthews, Mina O'Connell, Dale Oostdyk, Tim Oostdyk, Sister Renee and Janet Van Dyke. They were kind enough to read the material in its various forms. Their skills and sensitivities are reflected throughout this manuscript.

Without John Hayes and Scott Oostdyk the final version of the book would have been impossible. They spent weeks straightening out concepts and verb tenses that needed help. Most of all, they put their hearts into their efforts. Important parts of this book are theirs in both spirit and words.

The book was literally retyped for two years. Bev Hochradel patiently struggled through countless revisions and changes. Without her attitude and ability it is hard to imagine a written conclusion.

In February of 1981 the STEP Foundation was formed. Its executive committee consisted of Holly Coors, Mary Crowley, Arch Decker, E.V. Hill, Bunker Hunt, Kent Hutcheson, Clint W. Murchison, Jr., Robert Pittenger and Bud Smith. The board of the foundation played an important part in this presentation. Without their backing, many of the ideas would never have found living expression. Arch Decker's help was decisive because it was at the beginning. Jane and Bud Smith, Anne Murchison and Kent Hutcheson gave me unusual demonstrations of the living Christ. Robert Pittenger shared with me much discernment and encouragement. E.V. Hill's spoken words provided inspiration and his personal support was crucial. Without these friends, much of the last section of this document would not have been possible.

Family and friends contributed so much to this book. My mother, Hilda Oostdyk, taught me from a child by word and example to care for the needs of people. (... "for she has helped many in their needs, including me." Rom. 16:2) Hundreds of times my father, Engle Oostdyk, has helped me in my ministry to the poor. My brother John Oostdyk, often gave his concern beyond his responsibilities. My wife, Emily, participated in so much of the pain of my urban efforts and consistently demonstrated the compassion of

Christ to our children. My sons and daughters gave me so much encouragement and love.

I wish to extend appreciation to the Reverend Edward Danks, Howard
Annin and the Noroton Presbyterian Church of Darien, Connecticut who
believed before the evidence and were willing to take risks to help create it.
Also to Dr. Eugene S. Callender and the Church of the Master in Harlem who
were so much a part of the events of this book. I want to give special appreciation to Willie Mangham who is a son of the ghetto who lived.

I felt strongly that the material needed pictures. I have long been impressed with the skills and spirit of Rudy Vetter. Over the years he has
periodically come to visit our programs and to capture on film some of his
unique insights. Rudy's pictures have added much to the book.

I also want to acknowledge Dan and Viola Malachuk. They were willing to
publish a book which spoke to issues.

Finally, a special thanks to Mary Crowley—an unusual saint of God. Her life
is an inspiration and her generosity has ministered to many. She has been a
source of much encouragement to me.

FOREWORD

"Go through, go through the gates; prepare ye the way of the people; cast up, cast up the highway; gather out the stones; lift up a standard for the people."

Isa. 62:10

In order to understand this text, you have to understand the agrarian background of those who were fortunate enough to have been reared in the country. You must recognize that before you can do any successful farming, the land has to be cleared of all stone. You would not dare to put a pair of mules in a stony field. It would break them, the plow, and you. This is not easy work.

You and I live in a society where there are stones and rubble that have to be cleared out—pushers are not going to do it, pimps are not going to do it, stained glass windows are not going to do it, building a church and hanging a welcome sign isn't going to do it. You must have people who are willing to set a standard. When a field is cleared, make a furrow—every field has to have a perfect row. Once you get that perfect furrow, the whole field will have perfect rows. Isaiah said this is what we have to do. We've got to cast out, build up a highway, take out the stones and set a standard.

I state without fear of successful contradiction that the inner cities are the storehouses of explosive forces threatening our cities—indeed, our society—with destruction. I believe that the greatest thing that can be done to help the poor at this particular time in history is to improve the institutions that are responsible for ministering to their physical needs.

Every day there are approximately seventy-five institutions, agencies, programs, etc., designed to help one of the phases or aspects of the poor which come into my community of South Central in Los Angeles. I have served as chairman of the Poverty Committee under Mayor Yorty, chairman of the Los Angeles City Housing Commission, chairman of the Los Angeles City Fire Commission, and vice-chairman of the Los Angeles City Planning Commission. Also, I have been very active in community affairs, have organized many community projects, have built housing, plus pastored the Mount Zion Missionary Baptist Church. Based on my twenty years of experience it is my opinion that none of these agencies, institutions, or organizations are operating above thirty percent of their effectiveness nor accomplishing thirty percent of what they have been funded or designated to do.

Herein lies our problem and also our opportunity. If something could happen to the agencies designed to minister to my community such that their effectiveness was increased from thirty percent to eighty percent, I believe that the transformation which would result in the community would amount to passing from midnight to day.

One of God's yardsticks in judging any nation is based on how that nation helps the hurt and not the healed—how that nation blesses the poor and not how it rewards the rich. The poor may well remain with us always, but they do not have to remain sleeping on the streets. We may well have the poor with us always, but they need not always be hungry. Something and someone has to do it. My text calls for somebody that is somebody to do something. This is an age where God has equipped us to do something.

Therefore, my brethren, God has laid Lazarus at our gate once again. We have a great opportunity to demonstrate biblical Christianity.

We have little time to present our case.

PLEASE HURRY!

E.V. Hill
Pastor, Mount Zion Missionary
    Baptist church
President, World Christian
    Training Center
President, STEP Foundation

AN EXPLANATION

The word ghetto *is derived from the old Venetian word* geto *which means foundry. In the early 16th century, 5,000 Italian Jews lived on the site of an old abandoned foundry in Venice. The district was called Geto.*

Parade Magazine
November 30, 1980

This presentation often uses the word ghetto. Its use is meant to describe and not condemn. It is a forceful word. It is a poetic word. But it is also a negative word. May its use in these pages call attention to the plight of urban America, but it is not meant to reflect upon the worth of its citizens.

The translations used in this book are the New International Version (N.I.V.) and the Living Bible. All Scripture verses are in bold print. The Living Bible passages are italicized.

INTRODUCTION

This book took over twelve years to write. It started by accident. One day I was very depressed. I started to write some poems. It was a comfortable expression. Also a therapeutic one. For months and months I wrote poems about what had happened to me in Harlem. They just poured out: feelings found words and attracted more feelings and more words.

I then decided to see if I could write a book—a book of poems about Harlem. I planned to call it *White Mind*. It was to be about what happened to a suburban mind in the ghetto. I found out that sometimes a short poem could speak for a dozen pages of prose. But sometimes a long poem could not say what a few crisp sentences could. I could write poems about the sad and the glad but had less success with what lay in between where most of life is lived. So I gave up on *White Mind*. But from time to time I still wrote poems.

The Bible has always been an important book to me. Many days it was all I had. About four years ago I became excited by an idea. Why not take about a hundred of the most meaningful verses about the poor and write a poem about what they had to say and how it could apply to the ghetto? I began to take some of my old *White Mind* poems and match them up with Bible verses. Sometimes I just wrote new poems. Unfortunately, the total effect seemed fragmented so I abandoned that project, too. But every once in a while I'd write another poem about a Bible verse and the poor.

For many years I have worked on programs to bring help to urban America. I thought through ways in which the church could provide more meaningful help to the urban poor. After several decades of experimentation, failure and success, modification, evaluation and revision, I developed a plan that I felt would work. But only the church had the manpower and resources to implement it.

Two years ago I set my strategy out on paper and decided to see if I could weave my plan into my poems about the Bible verses. It all seemed to fit together. However, friends who read the manuscripts felt the strategy section should be isolated. I followed their advice and the plan read more clearly.

After reading the revised manuscript, my friends further suggested I isolate the poems that were mainly biblical insights away from the rest of the material. This seemed reasonable so I put all the biblical insights into their own section.

Finally, I acted upon a third criticism. One reader told me, "There is no hope in the book. I know you have participated in many urban break-throughs. But there are none in the book." I reflected upon this and realized that my friend was right. Although I had been involved in many urban victories, they had been so clouded by pain and difficulty that I had neglected to include them in my book. Many of these successes seemed like winning a war in which half of your friends were killed. I went back and put some of my war stories into the book. It wasn't too difficult to do. I simply dusted off some of my *White Mind* poems and tried to build a meaningful collage.

With the help of my friends I have finished the project. My book is divided into four sections. Section one is entitled *Profound Despair*. It attempts to give the reader a tour of the ghetto to become acquainted with some of its institutions, problems and people. Section two is called *Meaningful Hope*. This part chronicles my ghetto experience and attempts to suggest possibilities for bringing lasting change to the inner cities. Section three is called *Biblical Insights*. It attempts to share some truths about the poor from various scriptural passages. Finally, section four is entitled *A Specific Plan*. It outlines a strategy the churches can follow to help the poor.

Americans must begin to question thoroughly the role of government in delivering services to the poor. This is particularly timely since budget cuts in Washington dictate a reduced Federal role. The organized activities of concerned citizens should replace many existing government efforts such as job development, welfare, housing and legal assistance. These same caring individuals need to develop practical strategies to help improve those public and private institutions which will continue to provide services to the poor. For too long the urban teacher, policeman, nurse, etc., have had to labor alone. They must be supported.

In terms of both mission and resource, the Church is in the most advantageous position to mobilize Americans anxious to help. Ultimately, the problems of the ghetto are spiritual. The solution must also be spiritual. The whole concept of helping the poor is so difficult, the idea of re-structuring human service delivery systems and reshaping urban institutions so preposterous, that it can only be pursued by the grace of God.

> I AM the Lord,
> the God of all mankind.
> Is there anything too hard for me?"
> Jer. 32:27

PROLOGUE

I stood alone by the open casket. The makeup on the corpse unsuccessfully camouflaged the cause of death—ten bullets in the head.

I had known Bob Spivey well. He was a youth I met in Harlem eighteen years ago. He had no meaningful future. I helped him to go to college. I shared Christ with him. I shared my life. I cared for him. He cared for me. He was a leader. Because of him I got to know many of the sons and daughters of the ghetto. He came from where it doesn't matter, and now he was dead.

He died a street leader. But Harlem had pulled him to its lowest level. Great human potential was wasted. A child of God had died wrong.

I stood beside his body and grieved.

I recommitted myself to an unfinished task.

Contents

PROFOUND DESPAIR

It is the weakness of family structure, the presence of competing street values, and the lack of hope amidst affluence all around that make the American underclass unique among the world's poor people.

Rudolph Rauch
TIME
August 29, 1977

Lord, you know the hopes of humble people. Surely you will hear their cries and comfort their hearts by helping them. You will be with the orphans and all who are oppressed, so that mere earthly man will terrify them no longer.

Ps. 10: 17, 18

I have spent my entire adult life working in the ghetto. Each time someone has expressed interest in supporting or simply understanding my work, I have always suggested that they tour our projects. Few suburban people have seen the poorest sections of their city up close. Most middle and upper-class folks do not even know a single poor person. In fact, although materialism and racism most certainly perpetuate aspects of American poverty, I feel that there are two greater reasons why most folks have not significantly responded to urban need: their lack of exposure to poverty and to a meaningful plan to alleviate it. This book presents a plan; however, it will be easier to comprehend if the reader initially understands some things about the urban world of poverty.

The first section of this book, therefore, simulates a tour of the ghetto. In Harlem we took our guests around in vans. The reader will have to use my words and insights as his vehicle. Each entry paints a disturbing scene, introduces a broken life, speaks to an inner-city problem or simply recounts some of the frustrations one experiences living and working among the poor.

Many also share a verse of Scripture relevant to the topic.

The section has no thesis and it weaves no plot. It is a collection of images—an urban collage. It is designed to lend the reader eyes to see and ears to hear what he may not have encountered before.

1 A WHOLE LOT LEFT TO DO

. . . I stand amazed, silent, dumb with grief. Is there no medicine in Gilead? Is there no physician there? Why doesn't God do something? Why doesn't he help?

Jer. 8:21-22

during my years in the ghetto
I became a great walker of the streets
and the pacer of the pavements

soft sounds
on the cement
measured direction
releasing energy
the cadence of contemplation
the rhythm of thought

my street courses
were in decaying neighborhoods
endless blocks of neglect
mirroring each other
in dreadful reproduction
of the same old same old
abandoned buildings
forsaken people
wandering little kids
lingering junkies

constant walks into the night
marches into the winds of the season
with a quickening pace
hoping the velocity
would clear the mind

my emotional life
was like the shadows
reflected from the street lights
sometimes shining two ways at once
the one in the back wasn't finished
before the one in the front started
each competing for dominance
a desire to leave
a will to stay
like the crashing of a wave
and the resultant undertow
conflicting forces
producing tension
struggling for position

the succession of long walks
brought deep contemplation
about the nature of the ghetto
constant surveillance of the damage
raised the great inconsistencies
to a conscious level

a ghetto is a negative commentary
on our political system
an improper inventory of a free society
a result of somebody's selfishness
someone's lack of vigilance
over the responsibilities of freedom
no privilege can function
without corresponding obligations
no free society can possible survive
without ground rules
that is the only way to protect freedom
to sustain it
to refine it
freedom just can't mean
doing whatever you want
there must be a theory of others
some well-developed course of action
for helping those who have missed
there must be checks and balances
for a democracy to work
some consideration
for the philosophy of others
we can't leave that many people in need

their poverty
will force a free society
to either correct the inequalities
or proceed with repression

The People of the Ghetto

To walk the sidewalks of Harlem is to feel—beyond seeing or hearing it—the grip of desperation that has too many strong, healthy people sitting around for months at a time, waiting for jobs that will never materialize, looking for chances America now admits it cannot provide.

Clayton Riley

2 IMMOBILIZED

I went past the field of the sluggard, past the vineyard of the man who lacks judgment; thorns had come up everywhere, the ground was covered with weeds, and the stone wall was in ruins. I applied my heart to what I observed and learned a lesson from what I saw:

> a little sleep, a little slumber,
> a little folding of the hands to rest—
> and poverty will come on you like a bandit
> and scarcity like an armed man.
>
> Prov. 24:30-34

crowds form on the streets
crying out for dope and wine
broken lives huddled together
waiting for their fix
which won't fix nothing
huddled together
but together apart
going about the treacherous task
of hanging out
getting high
and screaming for new hustles
to keep getting higher
but for nothing
because joy has reached its lowest ebb
gladness has been banished from the land
time has little meaning on the streets
one day
is like another
an endless succession of sorrows

quenched only by what makes me high
so I can lose myself
in what doesn't matter
gladness is banned
and joy ebbs low
out of sight
lost

everyone is on one side of the street
as if the place has tilted
and all the people have slid into the shade

people
so many people
all sitting and standing around
it seems as though no one has left for work
as if this was the work
only it isn't work
like they have gotten used to it
have frozen the boredom
embalmed it
put it on display

a similar bar on the corner
the same crowd out front
stoops filled with bodies
like spectators
at a race track
the windows above mimicking bleachers
where more spectators
can watch the action below
and the action
is the same
day after day
a replica of yesterday
threatening to go on forever
like some evil curse
has sentenced them
to wait forever
to watch for nothing

3 A CONTEMPORARY ORPHAN

I became sincerely attached to a youth in Harlem named Ronnie Jones. He was the best young thief on the block. He was also seriously disturbed. This was clearly evident because he was perpetually in motion.

Ronnie was caught one day, but instead of being sent to jail he was placed in a mental hospital. I spoke to the authorities to explore the possibilities of his release. First I talked with his phychiatrist. Ronnie had a thick folder with his name on it revealing a dead prostitute for a mother, no known father, a series of foster homes and a life hopelessly tossed between a succession of rejecting experiences.

The doctor explained Ronnie's condition with this analogy: "Feelings are like fingers. If you expose them and they are constantly cut, then you begin to hide them because you don't want them hurt any more. Because of the constant rejection Ronnie faced, he withdrew his feelings to protect himself from further pain. He is now emotionally detached."

I wanted to help but the diagnosis was convincing. Ronnie had become a ghetto statistic created by neglect, sustained by indifference and assigned to Rockland State Hospital. Perhaps forever.

4   NEEDS OF THE NEEDY

For the needs of the needy shall not be ignored forever; the hopes of the poor shall not always be crushed.

Ps. 9:18

. . . "I know your one son died from an overdose of drugs and your other son is now on drugs, too. I'll talk to him again. But I don't know if it will do any good."

. . . "You're old. And you look out the window all day long. All you've got is your window and your TV. You want more. You deserve more."

. . . Turnip is on drugs and Karl is being seduced. Junkies don't like to shoot up alone; they are afraid of an overdose. The diabolical comradery of drugs, driven by necessity, spreads the curse.

. . . Hector is a child of disturbance and a son of uncertainty. He has a dubious beginning and a marginal future. Hector is incapable of consistency. His past has shaped a personality of distortion which is looking to somehow escape from the prison of himself. But each new effort only leads to frustration and compels him to inflict the pain of his confinement on himself and others.

. . . I'm not going back to college. I came home for Christmas vacation, the first time I have been back to Harlem since the end of the summer, and I found my family in disarray, especially my little brother. He's on drugs. Part of the reason I went to college was to be an example to my younger brothers and sisters—to give them something to copy. Well, I guess I was too far away and they got to be copying things closer at hand. Bad things. And they're all messed up. My little brother's a junkie, a miserable junkie. I'm dropping out of college. My heart's no longer in it. I just saw too much for Christmas. I'm not going back."

5   JUNKIES

junkies were everywhere
a permanent part of the landscape
as if some sinister presence
had done a huge seeding
and now they were sprouting up
everywhere

an intravenous nightmare
destroying from within
the will of so many
creating bondage
and slavery
and reducing personality
to distortion

the prevalence of drugs
was most blatant
on the street corners
in warm weather
junkies all over the place
doing their nod thing

bodies bobbing up and down
like an out of tune accordion
played slowly
by a senile old man
a cornerful of junkies
arranged like a perverse orchestra
in obedience to a secret maestro
beating out the sick time
in syncopated nods

obeying the silent commands
of their internal slavery

the human heartbreak was unfathomable
almost every family suffered
victims of a great plague
drugs fostered crime
released a ferocious appetite on the prowl
pitting the ghetto
against the ghetto
robbing from little
to produce less

the neighborhood had a multitude of problems
but some days it seemed as if
there was only one

6 THE STRENGTH OF THE GHETTO

Woe to the shepherds who feed themselves instead of their flocks . . . . I myself will be the shepherd of my sheep, and cause them to lie down in peace . . . . I will put splints and bandages upon their broken limbs and heal the sick.

Ezek. 34:1-23

to lots of folks
the ghetto
is home
don't want to leave
I like it here

the ghetto doesn't consist
of just winos
and drug addicts
and pimps
and prostitutes
and welfare cheats
and thieves

each block in the ghetto
has strong
reliable people
but these folks
have been overcome
by the rest

for every addict
there is a hard-working citizen
for every thief
there is a family man
for every welfare cheat

there is a woman
who because of the cruel cast of life
can only survive
because of that check
making the most
out of little
and teaching dignity
to her child

but we can't have
the stable part of a ghetto
carry the rest
because what happens is
it gets devoured instead
the junkies hang out on the corner
and won't move
the thieves rob their apartments
and no one can catch them
the welfare cheats
rob the dignity
of the poor lady
who needs it

the ghetto is the ghetto
because it is abandoned
and the saddest part of all
is the responsible poor
have to fight
almost alone
against all the rest

fight on brave stability
of the ghetto
you don't have much
but you still have your dignity
you haven't taken any handouts
but you get ripped off
by everybody else
passed by
and overlooked
but fight on
God loves you
somehow
and someday
maybe the people of God

will recognize your skills
and understand your plight
and surround you
with the needed support
and resources
and you will lead the drive
to clean up the ghetto

The Problems of the Ghetto

You have an education program, a welfare program, a day care program, a social service program, a mental hygiene program— all landing in communities like separate thunderbolts, as if they were dealing with different people. They are dealing, usually with similar families, with whole neighborhoods and whole communities. None of these programs, either administratively, legally, or bureaucratically, talk to one another.

Steven Berger

If this desk could talk

7 INSTITUTIONAL DEFICIENCIES

. . . . I will not leave them unpunished . . . For they have perverted justice . . . sold into slavery the poor who can't repay their debts; they trade them for a pair of shoes. They trample the poor in the dust and kick aside the meek.

Amos 2:6, 7

the institutions of the ghetto
don't create life
they foster dependency
which is to say
they foster death
they rob from potential
build in a standard of mediocrity
as if no one really cares
and what is at stake
is not that important

not that important to give extra homework
to solve a crime
to drive dope from the block
to clean a street
to create a job
to fix a park
to remove the abandoned car
to get an ambulance somewhere fast
to reduce the line in the emergency room
to tear down the abandoned building
to fix the street light

there are so many people
who work in the institutions
that serve the poor

yet this is the force
which destroys a ghetto
because too many of their staff
bring no expectation
to work with them
they perpetuate poverty
by their attitudes
they imprison the poor
assign them for life to the ghetto
they are the keepers of the poor
the sustainers of poverty
they get paid
to perpetuate the ghetto

our economy can't stand
such a loss of productivity
billions of dollars
being spent
to preserve poverty
this cycle must stop
and it must start
with the urban institutions
they must be restructured
to create and disperse
the development of people

"no longer" says the prophet Amos
"should they treat the poor
like an old pair of shoes
they trample the poor in the dust
and kick aside the meek
they have perverted justice
I will not leave them unpunished"

8   CRIME

I the Lord have called you to demonstrate my righteousness...
You shall also be a light to guide the nations unto me. You
will open the eyes of the blind, and release those who sit in
prison darkness and despair.

Isa. 42:6, 7

Crime on the streets is the urban issue of the eighties. It has become the substance of political rhetoric and newspaper headlines. The topic brings fear to the hearts of our citizens and our jails can no longer contain our prison population.

The ghetto breeds crime. Our jails are an extension of our streets. Blacks are imprisoned at a rate of 8.5 times that of whites. The prison population is now over 400,000 and growing at alarming rates. Only the Soviet Union and South Africa have greater incarceration rates. We just can't keep putting more and more people in jail. The fiscal burden will become intolerable. So will the human toll.

Once a youth from the streets told me, "The blindfolded woman holding the scales of truth is perhaps an accurate portrayal of ghetto justice. It would take someone blindfolded to create such a mess." Crime must be punished, but simply warehousing prisoners can't possibly be the solution. There is only one answer to prisons: reduce the source of the crime.

Respect given is often respect returned. If the Church went to urban America and eliminated some of the causes of poverty there would be fewer inmates in the jails. The prison population reflects a painful correlation to the churches' involvement in the ghetto.

It is suggested in Scripture that God meets us in the least of our brothers. Helping those in great need is an expression of our love to God.

...you have trampled and crushed beneath your feet the lowly
of the world and deprived men of their god-given rights and
refused them justice. ...

Lam. 3:34-36

9   ABANDONED BUILDINGS

there is a certain stench
that comes
from an abandoned building
as the wind blows
through the open front door
it's the bad breath
of the ghetto
an odor of stagnant death
block after block
of burned out
and forsaken structures
leave the senses dulled
suggesting a great human indiscretion
had been committed
and just to observe the results
was to somehow
participate in the guilt
the eerie silence
of an urban wasteland
that was somehow
more than silence
as if the silence demanded
to share its ugly tale
to explain in jarring detail
the deadly events
that had transpired
grotesque monuments
of rubble and ruins
gave deathlike evidence
of the cruel facts
that drove a people

from their land
an urban cemetery
of twisted bricks
a cause for self-examination
and urgent action
because the people who used to live there
now live somewhere else
replicating their patterns of destruction
a cycle conceived in neglect
so difficult to reverse

10 RACISM

Then God said, "Let us make man in our image, in our
likeness. . . ."

Gen. 1:26

how can an American society
write off people
because of some little things
nothing major
like hearts
or lungs
or legs
but the simple color
of skin

we were made
in the image of God
all of us
that is the important thing
that image reflects Him
that image is sacred
to reject his image
and substitute another
is racial idolatry
that is to worship
a man-made image

God made us all equal
but man did something distorted
with the human equation

the ghetto is the image of God
violated

11   NEGLECTED CHILDREN

But if anyone causes one of these little ones who believe in me
to sin, it would be better for him to have a large millstone hung
around his neck and to be drowned in the depths of the sea.

Matt. 18:6

Christ's attitude toward children
is very emphatic
if anyone hurts them
they should be drowned
in the depths of the sea

when I went to the ghetto
I was overwhelmed
by all the damage inflicted
upon all the little children

the young years
are the formative years
much of what a life becomes
is built into the beginnings

little helpless lives become
the ultimate horror statistic of the ghetto
raised without consistent nurture
subjected to not enough of so little
too often emotionally abandoned
in the oppressive weight
of urban survival

so few have participating fathers
and when you look closely
it is not that all the men were irresponsible

it's that the atmosphere of brokenness
is so extensive

let us not speak too loudly
in our condemnation of the ghetto father
because somehow we have stripped him
of his manhood
condemned him for not performing
with what we took away

the urban woman
is too often left to do her parenting alone
surrounded by every possible obstacle
in the midst of
so much poverty
she is left to survive
and often she goes under
subjected to the same cruel forces as her man
some make it better than others
but most lose
when they let their little children outside to play
it's all over the streets
it's in the air
the temptations and obstacles are too great
most of the young lives get damaged

the people in jail
the ones strung out on dope
the ones that dropped out of school
the ones not making it
how did it get to be that way

the young years
are spent amid emotional havoc
and the desperate attempts by those giving the love
to somehow make it themselves
the pressures build
everything becomes so impossible
that people break
and they just die inside
begin to accept the givens

the real tragedy of the ghetto
is that some people begin to believe it
internalize it
and attempt to raise children amidst it

abandoned children
raised by abandoned people
amid so much wrong

all the conditions
that make the ghetto
the ghetto
collect in a stagnant pool
and become the stuff
that too many little street kids
are raised on
like the umbilical cord is corrupted
and all the tragic evil
is fed intraveneously
this destructive process must stop
cut the cord
sever the thing for God's sake
but what have you got to replace it
name your alternatives

we want to correct the problem
and yet we are often the source
because in many ways
the polluter of the umbilical cord
is us

12   EDUCATIONAL DISADVANTAGE

... Oh Lord, the poor man trusts himself to you; you are known as the helper of the helpless.

Ps. 10:14

I ask the question
over and over again
why aren't the youths from the ghetto
going to college
in suburbia it was assumed most would go
on the streets it was assumed most would not

who is responsible
for this insane edict
who can you go see
to change it

the urban students are programmed to fail
by teachers and guidance counsellors
who assume the kids can't
so they don't

it is all pre-arranged
urban predestination
a fiat
based upon
where you grow up
because there is no one
with authority
to rechannel the flow
to personally challenge the formula

to whisper in the ear of the child
that you have a future

there is hope
do this
and this
and this

to shout in the ear of the system
this is my son
I want
I insist
that you do this
and this
and this·

alienated from
guidance
direction
encouragement
so many
of the sons and daughters of the streets
are mass produced
into functional illiterates
programmed to fail
and rationalized under the premise
that these are kids from the ghetto

13   THE BY-PRODUCTS OF POVERTY

Yes, the glory of Israel will be very dim when poverty stalks the land.

Isa. 17:4

- the light-skinned boy sits opposite me, his head bowed in deep dejection. So much pain and sadness has already been crammed into his eighteen years. He has made two girls pregnant. He plans to marry one and is desperately trying to secure money for an abortion for the other.

- the tall boy is hanging over the desk expressing himself with unusual authority, telling me his deepest thoughts. He had just taken his first mainline shot of heroin. He is screaming at me about how he had always felt inferior but now he felt nice. "Now you can pay attention to me 'cause now I am a bad guy."

- the young man has deep psychological problems. He is in love with a girl several months pregnant. The baby is not his. The relationship has met mutual needs but it is obviously headed for greater tragedy.

- the scene is the bathroom. Towels and two belts hang on the rack. I rip the belts down in disgust because I know their use—a temporary tourniquet to set up the deadly heroin injection.

- he is sitting on the stoop telling me about his afternoon disappointment. His father, whom he has not seen for seven years, recently called to make an appointment to see him. He waited for two hours. His father never came. It is one of those sacred times when all I can do is listen.

14   PEOPLE OF LITTLE EFFORT

Let me sleep a little longer! Sure, just a little more! And as you sleep, poverty creeps upon you like a robber and destroys you. . . .

Prov. 6:10, 11

When a nation ignores their God and his commandments, his displeasure is not limited to the rich and powerful. His judgment is also directed toward the poor.

Many of the problems of an American ghetto are caused by the people who live there—or rather some of the people who live there. You do not need to sell dope on your block. You do not have to spend endless days sitting on the stoop of your building doing nothing. You don't have to drink wine and be high all day. You can look for a job or a better job. You can try to organize your block no matter what the odds. You don't have to have another baby when you're not married and can't take care of the three you already have. You don't have to take a cab or buy a new pair of shoes if there is something better you can do with the money.

The ghetto has many Christians. There is no reason why there is not far better organization and growth. So much can be changed when even a few determined souls decide that it is time for action. But in most cases, even rudimentary efforts have not been made.

It is not always rich folks who deserve the judgment of God. Often it is a lot of poor folks as well.

15   MORE THAN WORDS AND MONEY

If I gave everything I have to poor people, and if I were burned alive for preaching the Gospel but didn't love others, it would be of no value whatever.

I Cor. 13:3

the deepest need of the ghetto
is personalism

come care for me
and let me care for you
know my name
and let me know yours
watch what I do
and let me watch you
ask me questions
as I question you
love me
as I love you

the problems of the ghetto
cannot be solved
by money alone
there is too much
money can't buy

you just can't throw
money at a ghetto
and say live

the problems of the ghetto
can't be solved
by just preaching the gospel

doctrine without performance
is words
the ghetto doesn't need
any more words
even gospel words

the ghetto needs love
but love must take
the form of justice

there is love in the ghetto now
that's why there's hurt and anger
when you love your son
or love your wife
or love your mother
it hurts you
to see all the things
they can't have
because of injustice

if people want to love me
then stop the dope
from coming into my community
do something about my heat
about the abandoned building next door
about my daughter's reading level
about the jail my son is in

love makes a great teacher
love changes a jail
love makes a faithful landlord
love is understanding in the courtroom
love shortens the waiting time in the emergency room
love changes a policeman's attitude
love creates volunteers

keep your money oh rich church
I need more than tithes
toss your collection plates
in the air
spin them
through the sanctuary
spewing their contents
back into the pews
don't need your money
I need you

your faithfulness to Christ
come care for me
like you care for yourself
that's what the Bible says anyway
that you love me
like you love God

I'm your neighbor
I live here in the ghetto
and you forgot all about me

so stop your preaching
it's an insult to my ears
words can't heal the ghetto
for God so loved the world
that He gave us a ghetto
how can there be a ghetto
with millions of Christians
blasphemy
blasphemy
you don't love me
or you wouldn't leave me with this
and then you preach the love of God
you ain't got that love
if all you got is words

and the ghetto goes on
and so do the words

but the Word became flesh
and dwelt amongst us

Christian Responsibility for the Ghetto

The city lies in chaos, every home and shop is locked up tight to keep out looters. Mobs form in the streets, crying for wine; joy has reached its lowest ebb; gladness has been banished from the land. The city is left in ruins; its gates are battered down.
Isa. 24:10-12

Today many who name the name of Christ have removed themselves from human hurt and suffering to places of relative comfort and safety. Many have sought to protect themselves and their families from the poor and the wretched masses for whom Christ showed such primary concern. . . . The church's compassionless inactivity stems from being removed and out of touch with the suffering of the poor and the exploited.
Jim Wallis

16   MEETING PLACES

When a Samaritan woman came to draw water, Jesus said to her, "Will you give me a drink?" (His disciples had gone into the town to buy food.) The Samaritan woman said to him, "You are a Jew and I am a Samaritan woman. How can you ask me for a drink?" (For Jews do not associate with Samaritans.)

John 4:7-9

Jesus asked a Samaritan woman for a drink. The Jews and Samaritans didn't speak to each other. Deep hostility existed between them. Neither did men and women speak to each other publicly in those days.

A Jewish man was asking a Samaritan woman for a drink. He was meeting her at her level. It was only a matter of time before He was talking to her at his.

When I was a young boy I got very excited one Sunday morning over an announcement by the minister. He was asking for volunteers to come and help put up the tent for an evangelist who was coming into the area. The whole thought of tents fired the imagination of a child.

I asked my daddy if I could go with him to watch the big event. I will never forget approaching the project and becoming hysterical with laughter because it was the first time in my life I had seen men of the church in their old clothes. They all looked so comical in their overalls.

And why hadn't I ever seen the men of my church in their old clothes? It was because everything we ever did that was called "Christian" required a shirt and tie.

If the Church ever rolled up its sleeves and went to the ghetto, it would be seen in a whole new light. In turn, it would also see the poor in a new light.

Christ met the woman at the well. That is where she was. The Church needs to meet the poor in the ghetto. There we can all talk about living water. We all need it.

17 TOUCHED BY JESUS

A large crowd followed and pressed around Him. And a woman was there who had been subject to bleeding for twelve years. She had suffered a great deal under the care of many doctors and had spent all she had, yet instead of getting better she grew worse. When she heard about Jesus, she came up behind him in the crowd and touched his cloak, because she thought, "If I just touch his clothes, I will be healed." Immediately her bleeding stopped and she felt in her body that she was freed from her suffering.

Mark 5:24-29

his little voice broke the silence of the night
"water
water"

the small boy
had been asking for a drink
so often
of late

his request
was always granted
but some quiet questionings
were beginning to come
about the frequency
of his demands

then this particular night
the cry was so unusually piercing
and the water gulped down
with such intensity
that something
just had to be wrong

the medical diagnosis
revealed that
an ineffective pancreas
was not secreting
enough insulin
causing a serious imbalance
of the body's chemistry

while water
would temporarily silence
his cries
it was not satisfying his real needs
he needed insulin
not water

the deepest needs
of the human heart
cannot be met by things
the answer to life
is not the elimination of poverty
but to know Christ

though isn't it rather strange
that some Christians want to share Christ
with the poor
but don't want to share
much of anything else

but if Christians don't help the poor
who will ever believe
that Christ is worth sharing

18 BEGGARS AT THE DOOR
OF THE CHAIRMAN

There was a rich man who was dressed in purple and fine linen and lived in luxury every day. At his gate was laid a beggar named Lazarus, covered with sores. . . .

Luke 16:19-31

A rich man and a beggar at the same front door. The rich man owned it and Lazarus was begging there.

Our society has dramatically cut down on the number of beggars. They are now taken care of by the Salvation Army or missions or welfare. But the poor still go begging—only at different doorsteps.

However, the responsibility of the rich to the poor has not been removed, but only shifted. The powerful people of our society are in control of the political and charitable boards that help the poor. But these structures are largely ineffective. The responsibility for this lies with the influential people who control them.

Once I remember seeing the chairman of the board of a large American corporation. We began to talk about his involvement with the poor.

The man opened his drawer and took out two lists. One recorded all the organizations of which he was presently a part. The other consisted of what he had turned down in the past few months.

I stared at the lists in amazement. The influence the man had was overwhelming.

I looked at him, took a deep breath and started in. "Sir, I sit here on my side of your office knowing so much about the ghetto. I have so many ideas about what to do. But I have no power. I sit on no boards. You sit on your side of your office knowing very little about the ghetto. But you sit on the boards of so many organizations which control the destiny of the poor. That is the dilemma. I represent ideas and you represent influence, but our two worlds seldom intersect."

I continued, "Dynamic help for the ghetto will only come when our two symbolic chairs can come together. Yet this great gulf remains between us.

66

I'm powerless to bridge it and your lists are all filled."

I knew that I hadn't said it very well and the man looked at his watch as if he were late for a meeting. So I thanked him for his time and got up to leave wishing I could be the board chairman just for a little while.

The passage from Luke suggests that the story does not end at the rich man's doorstep. It ends in judgment in the afterlife. God holds the rich responsible for what happens on their doorstep. He will also hold them responsible for what happens on their boards.

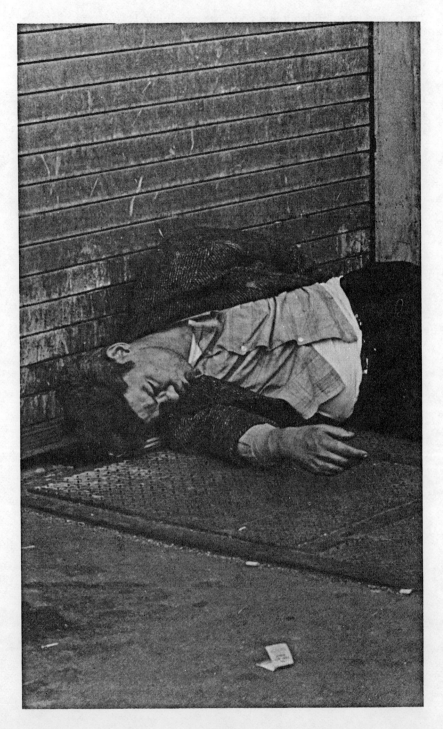

19   NEW AGENDAS

.... and the church had
its annual meeting
there was a good feel in the air
it had been a good year
report after report
seemed to confirm growth
the new building was done
a fund drive for a new organ was about to begin
the Sunday school had its best year
the choir had bought new robes
the budget was larger than ever
the charismatic conference made a deep impact
in the midst of the progress
a young man arose
from the back of the room
and quietly began to read
a passage of Scripture

*I hate your show and pretence—your hypocrisy of 'honoring'
me with your religious feasts and solemn assemblies. I will not
accept your burnt offerings and thank offerings. I will not
look at your offerings of peace. Away with your hymns of
praise—they are mere noise to my ears. I will not listen to your
music, no matter how lovely it is. I want to see a mighty flood
of justice—a torrent of doing good.*

Amos 5:21-24

when the young man was finished
he sat down
it was very quiet in the room
as if a car had been shifted into reverse

while it was still going forward
or as though death had invaded the party

the alert minister
asked for a period of silence
for everyone to pray to God

then he asked the young man
to read the passage again

20   INDIFFERENCE TO HUMAN NEED

While in Capernaum Jesus went over to the synagogue again, and noticed a man there with a deformed hand ... Since it was the Sabbath, Jesus' enemies watched him closely. Jesus asked the man to come and stand in front of the congregation. Then turning to his enemies He asked, "Is it all right to do kind deeds on Sabbath days? ..." But they wouldn't answer him. Looking around at them angrily, for he was deeply disturbed by their indifference to human need, he said to the man, "Reach out your hand." He did, and instantly his hand was healed!

Mark 3:1-6

Jesus was angry
he was deeply disturbed
by their indifference
to human need

a man with a deformed hand
was used to having people stare at him
and now he was up there
in front of all those people
and they were staring at him
and at Jesus

but the issue
was not his twisted hand
it was what day it was

my hand
my sad hand
the one I always try to hide
the one I can't use
the one my mother cried over

71

I cry over
and now this Jesus
wants to heal it
and these people
are concerned about
what day it is
heal it Jesus
don't worry about their sick rules

I want to play ball
and hold a girl's hand
and I'll pray to you
with both hands
so everyone can see
my two hands
together
together
Jesus please
heal my hand

people had put religion
ahead of human need
rules over mercy
regulation over concern

one of the difficulties
of the ghetto
is that no one sees it
the withered lives of poverty
are unsafely tucked away
miles from where most people live
the Christian community must come up with a plan

helping the ghetto
without a plan
usually leads to paternalism
band-aids
cleaning back yards
painting stoops

the ghetto has much to teach
but not once a year
on clean-up day

the Church needs to take a long look
at the problems of the poor
call them up before us Jesus

and let us look
at what we have allowed to happen

we have the skills
but we have been caught up
in our own indifference
distracted by T.V.
and church choirs
and dinner parties
and automobiles
and being busy
and theological arguments

but Jesus
lead us past our mistakes
and turn us to our task
allow us to heal the hurt
and fix the ghetto

and dear God
heal us
because the ghetto
became the ghetto
because we the healers
were sometimes the creators
and in the recognition of that fact
our paternalism dies
on the altar of obedience
and we rise cleansed
to help the ghetto

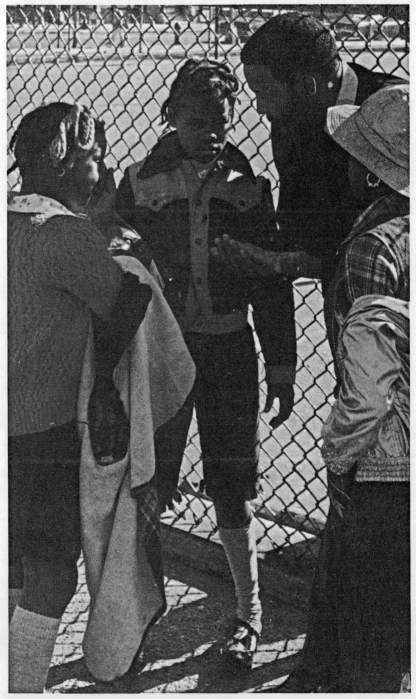

Meaningful hope

Section Two
MEANINGFUL HOPE

Because my mouth is wide with laughter you do not hear my inner cry? Because my feet are gay with dancing you do not know I die?

Langston Hughes

Your sons will rebuild the long-deserted ruins of your cities, and you will be known as, "The People who Rebuild Their Walls and Cities."

Isa. 58:12

Tours are always an important source of knowledge. They allow us to see things firsthand. But the tourist's perspective is basically superficial. Sometimes it is essential to live in a place to fully understand it.

I have spent my whole adult life in the ghetto. Many of the impressions I formed as a suburban youth have been reshaped by the realities of the streets in which I lived and worked. But I did more than labor in a ghetto. I tried to help change it. I pursued impossible dreams and the results became many difficult experiences. I want to share a slice of these years with the reader in the hope that it will broaden his understanding of the ghetto. This crucial background is needed to bring clearer focus to the rest of the book.

21 SIMPLE BEGINNINGS

In the mid 50's I started working for a Christian youth organization called Young Life. This group had an action-oriented ministry. We first attempted to befriend young people by spending time with them where they were—in pool halls, on athletic fields or outside candy stores. Eventually we would organize a weekly meeting in someone's home where kids sang songs, laughed at humorous skits and heard a short message about Jesus Christ. I found Young Life to be an attractive vehicle for the expression of my faith. But a conflict soon began to grow in my mind. Young Life was only working with suburban youth. I felt we needed a greater urban presence. Since Newark, New Jersey, was closest to my home, I first focused my efforts to help the poor there.

Young Life should not be especially faulted for its suburban bias. Its attitude about urban things paralleled that of most institutions. They all seemed to be on the same "white" agenda. I guess that is how the Harlems got to be Harlems.

I came to know a lot about the ghetto because of Vinnie Pasquale. He lived in a poor section of Newark. The leader of an Italian street gang, Vinnie looked much older than his years. He had spent time in jail and had a bad drug habit. He was very lost.

For one whole summer I shared my life and faith with Vinnie, building a relationship with him. Vinnie asked Jesus Christ to come into his life. It was a significant start but it was only a beginning. I shared the Scriptures with him and taught him about growing in Christ.

Although Vinnie was twenty-two, he had almost never worked. He promised to get a job. But then Vinnie was sent to jail for a crime he had committed before he became a Christian. He swore that five thousand dollars to his lawyer would buy him the right judge but I didn't want to participate in that. Vinnie deteriorated in jail. It was a difficult place for a new Christian to grow in his faith.

When Vinnie got out of jail it was all efforts to nowhere. He never got that

78

job and he went back on drugs. Because I had invested so much time into Vinnie, I kept trying to reach him. I cared for the man and I wanted him to make it. But finally I realized that Vinnie couldn't make it through my effort. He had to make it through his. I left him in God's hands, telling him, "Vinnie, whenever you're ready, you know my phone number."

Months passed and all I could do for Vinnie was pray. Then one day the phone rang. It was Vinnie. He was tired of his life. The previous night he had prayed for God's help. He was ready.

Vinnie got a job in a YMCA. He joined a church. A dedicated assistant minister gave him a lot of help. There was exciting progress.

In time Vinnie asked if he could go back to school. He was a ninth-grade dropout who wanted to pursue an education. I arranged for him to attend an accelerated prep school and two years later he graduated. Soon Vinnie started college. He met a wonderful woman and got married. His wife became pregnant and Vinnie looked forward to the great event.

Then late one night Vinnie telephoned. The baby had been born, but with birth defects. I was angry. Here was a promising golden glove fighter from a broken home whose life had been wrecked by drugs and crime. He had overcome so much and had gone on to school, graduated, married, and had brought a new life into the world. But instead of a normal birth, there were problems. The joy of that experience was marred. It didn't seem fair. When Vinnie sensed my frustration, he softly said to me, "Harv, I don't know why babies aren't born perfect. But if it has to happen to anyone it was probably best it happened to me. I have been through so much bad, I can handle this. I can love my little daughter anyway. Maybe some people couldn't." My only response was tears.

Vinnie Pasquale never finished college nor did he return to work in the ghetto. He moved to the New Jersey shore where he got a job as a janitor in a junior high school.

One day I received another phone call. Vinnie Pasquale was dead. He had died of a heart attack while playing basketball with some of the students.

I loved Vinnie and now he was gone. I sat and thought about him for a long time. His life had been somewhat of a disappointment to me. I had wanted him to achieve more. But I knew that the beauty of Vinnie was not in what he became, but what he hadn't become. He could have spent his life destroying others and himself: taking things from others rather than giving, wasting tax dollars as he wasted in prison, producing children who were unwanted and uncared for, excluding God from all aspects of his life.

Vinnie had held a marriage together. He had loved his children. He had kept a job. Vinnie had died playing basketball with some students he cared about. He had died as Christ had taught him to live—caring about others. I had learned so much about poor people through Vinnie. The teacher had been taught.

Vinnie Pasquale ministers to a youth

22   A WHOLE LOT OF SADNESS

Each of us has dreams and aspirations. They shape our lives and foster our activities. Some people want to be rich or to have a yacht; others to drink beer and watch TV. As head of Young Life in the New York area, I hoped to combine urban and suburban areas, tenements and split levels, grass and cement, cars and subways, Scarsdale and Harlem. I wanted to trade off the resources of suburbia with the needs of the ghetto and have the whole process become a symbol of God's redemptive love. This was my great dream, one worthy of being acted upon. Beginning in the early sixties, I went to Harlem.

walking through Harlem
you knew the next block
would be like the last block
only the bar
would be on the corner
rather than in the middle of the block
next to the fish and chips
instead of the hair dresser
or the abandoned building
what you saw
was what you expected
each block was a microcosm
of the ghetto
what you no longer expected
no longer was
each store had iron gates
like beat up eyelids
during the day
the eyelids never seemed open all the way
and at night
they all closed real tight

81

life in the ghetto
destroys some people
drives them to become junkies
winos
drifters
others it resigns to mediocrity
content with the mundane
to wake up each day
and accept
the defined perimeters of an existence
it becomes the given
the chant of life
the limits of achievement
some perverse formula
accepted as dogma
some absurd equation
embraced as truth
limiting
confining
dictating

from this reservoir
comes the domestic
who cleans offices and homes
the pusher of garment trucks
the parker of cars
and the thousands of other menial workers
doing jobs
that no one else wants to do
working hard each day
hoping the best for their children
they are the backbones
of churches
the numbers rackets
customers
for hairdressers
undertakers
citizens who provide stability
the sea of faces in the subway
the glue of the ghetto
living out their lives
within the confines of the given

    • he had a bullet in his arm
      it was now three days

since it happened
he said it was an accident
didn't want to elaborate
said it hurt bad
he wanted some money
to see a doctor
his kind of doctor
his kind of secret
about his kind of bullet

• the baby died
maybe it was for the best
they sat in a crowed room
comforting themselves
sharing better the baby's death
than they had the child's life
the room was filled
with assorted friends and relatives
all avoiding the other room
in which a dead baby
lay on an empty bed
services are bad in the ghetto
whether it is your garbage
or your mail
you must wait
ambulances don't come very fast
coroners don't either
it was six hours
before the city got around
to make official
what already was

• he died of an overdose
of heroin
he was dead for three days
before anyone knew
a youthworker found him on the floor
of his rented room
where he had lived alone
no one that young
should be dead
that long
without anyone
knowing

each day started for me
with morning sickness
as though I had fallen victim
to a strange pregnancy
and the pain in my stomach
just wouldn't go away
the demands of the task
were absolute
like building sandcastles
in the swirling winds of the Sahara
or bailing out a boat
during the driving monsoon
the problems and pressures
began expressing themselves
in successive layers of the impossible
I summoned all kinds of energy
to respond to each new difficulty
completely concentrating on the present
determined to bring meaning out of the chaos

late one night I separated myself
for my survival
too tired to try anymore
arriving home
I found a note
wishing me a happy anniversary
some simple words
expressing profound pathos
I retreated out into the June night
to reflect on what I had forgotten
it was a beautiful evening
Harlem seemed so far away
so unreal
so unnecessary
I began to wonder
if the costs of the effort
were beginning to extract
too high a price
what else would I forget to remember
or would I soon be remembering to forget
a troubled soul
on a serene night
conjuring up enough courage
to wake up a woman
he had forgotten

23 CROSSING BARRIERS

Jesus answered, "I am the way and the truth and the life."

John 14:6

38 *DAILY NEWS, WEDNESDAY, JUNE 17, 1964* **##**

Leap to Escape Police Kills Purse Snatcher, 15

By WILLIAM TRAVERS and WILLIAM RICE

Kenneth Bellinger, 15, of 352 W. 118th St., took a foolish gamble last night. He staked his life against the contents of a woman's purse—and lost.

The youth died in Metropolitan Hospital two hours after he had plunged from a roof while fleeing the cops.

This was Kenneth's gamble, as told by the police:

Shortly after 7 P.M. Kenneth saw Lorraine Rettig, 33, a secretary at Flower and Fifth Ave. Hospitals, walking on 110th St. toward the Eighth Ave. subway. He also saw her purse.

Pal Retrieves Purse

He snatched it and, as the woman screamed, began to run. In his haste he dropped the handbag, which quickly was retrieved by a second youth who sped away with Kenneth.

Although the boys didn't know it, the purse was worthless to them. When it dropped, the woman's wallet popped out.

A passerby, Robert Brown, 45, heard Miss Rettig's screams, saw the fleeing youths and gave chase. He pursued them toward Seventh Ave. and through an alley leading to 111th St.

Cops Take Up Hunt

There, Brown lost the boys but found Patrolmen John Taylor and Louis Pulliam of the W. 123d St. station, who were passing in a prowl car. Told of the incident, Taylor put in a call for help. Pulliam ran to the roof of 238 W. 111th St. on a hunch that the boys might take to the rooftops. He was right. Three buildings away he spotted the boy with the purse. The patrolman ordered him to halt and fired three warning shots. At that moment he saw Kenneth on the roof of 247 W. 111th St., across the street.

Boy Leaps, Misses

Again Pulliam yelled halt-and fired a couple of shots into the air. Kenneth ran to the edge of the roof, eyed the roof of 245 W. 111th St., about six feet away, and leaped.

He missed and plunged five stories to the alleyway below. The other boy got away. Brown identified the fatally injured Kenneth as one of the boys who had snatched the purse. Police said the youngster had had three previous brushes with the law, two involving purse snatches and another involving a robbery.

Dear Friend,

For the past ten days two of our young black leaders and I have been attempting to make friendships on a Harlem playground. Almost immediately, Kenny Bellinger, who was the obvious leader of the crowd, responded to us. We talked to him about the possibilities of going to Colorado and on Monday, after a weekend of talking with his friends, he brought us a list of 12 boys who wanted to go to the ranch. Late Tuesday afternoon we walked off the playground together: Kenny to his death and three leaders to deep disappointment.

Kenny jumped and missed; perhaps a symbolic act that represented the basic direction of most of the young lives of Harlem. The woman's purse was empty; the act senseless; perhaps symbolic once again of the purposelessness that pervades the atmosphere of the nation's largest ghetto.

Kenny died a useless death; 2000 years ago Christ died a death that should have prevented Kenny's. The tragedy seems to lie in the fact that Kenny died two weeks before he might have discovered this.

Kenny Bellinger can't go to Colorado this summer; but 90 teenagers from various inner-city sections of our Metropolitan area can. Each one has to pay $30. The remaining must come from concerned people.

Kenny had rounded up 12 disciples of need; we left them today sitting stunned on the stairways of Harlem.

All that stands between them and possible help is a purse given, not stolen.

We urgently need your help.

Yours Sincerely,

Harv Oostdyk

Harv Oostdyk

24   THE CHURCH WALL

Dr. Eugene Callender was the pastor of Harlem's Church of the Master. He had the rare ability to go off in two directions at the same time and manage both efforts. He knew the ghetto but he also knew how to talk to white folks. That tenuous balance was hard to achieve in the early sixties. Dr. Callender accepted our Young Life program and helped to shepherd it through some of the difficulties that a vital street project would encounter. Because of his backing, I agreed to develop a strong youth program for the church. In addition to the sanctuary, the church owned a brownstone next door. That building became the nerve center of the program.

> sometimes in the history of architecture
> and design
> things become
> what they were not meant to be
>
> the Church of the Master had a wall
> a simple structure of brick and mortar
> constructed as a small barrier
> on one side of the building
>
> with the growth of the program
> the top of the wall
> had become a bench
> on whose surface
> continually
> sat the youth of Harlem
>
> it was the spot to be
> a hang-out
> a collecting place
> where you found out what was happening
> and why
> and by whom
> and for what reason
> and when
> and so on
>
> the whole spectrum of human experience
> was expressed on those bricks
> a place that promised some attention
> to destroy some boredom
> a whirlpool of emotion
> churning
> to hear

to tell
to feel a part of things
to find love
to express hate

kids sat there
depressed
happy
sad
high
perplexed
or just in neutral

they slept on its top
urinated on its sides
wrote on its face
smoked pot
were counseled
made love to
planned robberies
prayed
the guts of life were constantly spewed out
a canvas of Harlem
expressed through warm bodies
sitting on a wall

like a sponge on water
or ants on crumbs
the crowd constantly collected there
usually dozens
sometimes hundreds

25 THE GOSPEL AND THE GHETTO

When Jesus spoke it was in the idiom of the people. He talked of wheat and mustard seeds and the people understood. All great communication must be in the language of the hearers. Each Wednesday night a large crowd gathered in the small basement gym of the Church of the Master. It was my task to convert concepts and feelings about the Gospel into words that could be understood by the youth of Harlem.

I had spoken to hundreds of audiences
but talking to Harlem
was a difficult experience
before my new congregation
I felt like I was stuttering
this was the ultimate communicative challenge
sound waves bouncing back
undelivered
vocal cords straining to say it right
but getting only distress signals

communicating to the Harlem crowd
presented more than just cultural obstacles
some of the crowd was always
coming and going
a large portion of the youth were high
potential interruptions abounded
constantly threatening to unravel the meeting
but unmistakably openness prevailed
barriers were down
the looks in most of the faces
conveyed willingness
to explore further
to share

to expose
to discover

yet I strongly felt
my middle class answers
were too much there
too close to the surface
like a can of paint
not yet mixed
not yet fit for spreading
but necessity
demanded a beginning
ready or not here they come
speak

what I had been telling myself
and others
for years
about life
about Christ
didn't seem to apply on the streets
my timing was off
soon it affected my confidence
unable to express with conviction
I spoke less
because I was no longer sure

not frightened by the truth in Christ
just the translation of it
my speeches
seemed prepared
for another day
another location

gradually
my inclination
was to move from verbal proclamation
to action
something I could be more sure of
get my hands on
acts to be identified as Christ-like
so I struggled at serving
a day in court
listening to a heart cry out
getting youth back into school
fixing up a building

such acts expressed obedience to the Gospel's commands
and were a natural expression of God's love

except
with my whole heart
I wanted to cry out
expressing a deeper answer
than education
health
housing
but words stuck in my throat
like an infant
struggling to say what he means
confined
to sounds
and gestures

in my silent confusion
I wanted to stammer out
scream
holler
yell
until the deep issues
were probed
the frantic level
survival
visceral
the loneliness of the soul
the guilt of the heart
the fear of the unknown
the mystery of death
the hurt of rejected love
the hunger for acknowledgment
the need of forgiveness
the desire to know God

I knew Christ was the solution
but how could I shape the answer
for the ghetto
the wool kept coming off the ball
the onion just kept peeling
definition was needed
explanations
reasons
little children fatherless

functional illiterates
heroin
abandoned buildings
abandoned women
hate
racism
another copped plea
rhetoric
filth
incarceration to nowhere
stolen welfare checks
and so on

however
I knew if social conditions
were exemplary in the ghetto
and racism had been forever driven
from the face of the continent
the human heart would still be restless
exploring unfulfilled desires
welling up in one's insides
demanding to be fulfilled

I knew
because I had been a part
of affluent white America
and the deepest answers weren't there
that's why I had believed in Jesus
in the first place
because being white
and accepted
and affluent
and gifted
and having a future
and the rest of the agenda
wasn't enough

the truth in Christ
that came crashing into human history
through the incarnation
is what excited me
had touched my whole life
what I wanted to share
the Christ who spoke of life
who addressed Himself

to the ultimate questions of human existence
in an appropriate way

one day
at a well
Jesus asked a Samaritan woman for a drink
more to meet her needs than his

"If only you knew what God gives
and who it is that is asking for a drink,
you would have asked Him
and He would have given you living water"

"Sir," the woman said, "you have no bucket
and this well is deep"

Jesus said, "Everyone who drinks this water
will be thirsty again
but whoever drinks the water that I shall give him
will never suffer thirst anymore
the water that I shall give him
will be an inner spring always welling up for eternal life"
Jesus had addressed human need
with relevant words

in the urban milieu
the necessity for answers is always accelerated
because the needs are so expansive
so desperate
so complex

under the load
I staggered
looking for props
something to hold on to
I suddenly realized
I had no course to follow
no archetype
no model
no plan
and turning around
I screamed out
to my informal audience
in the overcrowded Harlem gym

"I don't have
all the answers yet

but what I have
I give sincerely
in the name of the Father
and Son
and the Holy Ghost
Amen"

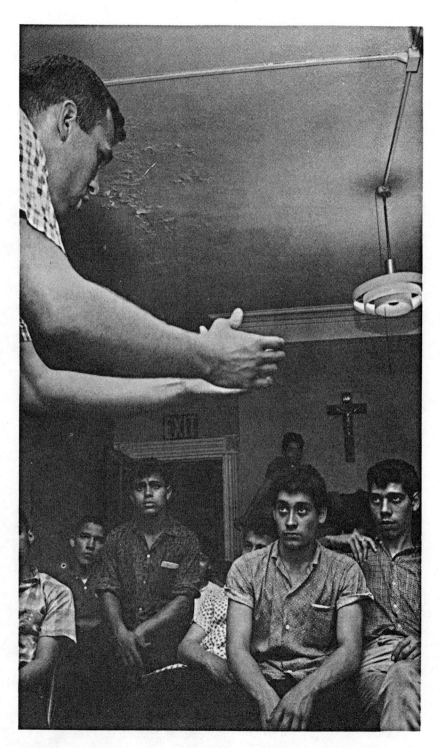

26 SOME ROOMS ON THE STREETS

In time I came to realize that if I was to succeed in the ghetto I needed to isolate some of the leaders of the streets to focus on their need. These were dynamic young men who had larger-than-life reputations and vast followings among their peers. They had the potential to bring about great change. Jesus worked with twelve. I rented two apartments on one floor and moved in to share some of my life with a half a dozen of Harlem's favorite sons.

the fellows affectionately
called the apartments
Yakka Flats
I suppose there was some reason
but I can't remember why

I was the captain in my foxhole
marshalling my meager resources
mobilizing every conceivable facility
of the human spirit
for a determined effort
towards survival
instilling encouragement
strategy
on an hour-to-hour basis
crawling for inches
fighting fiercely for small things
attempting to build a winning attitude
refusing under any condition to surrender

life in the apartment
began early each morning
getting the fellows off to school
and then it was off to minister to needs
"please go to court with me"

"I want to kick my habit"
"my mother is desperately ill"
the constant beat of need
in the arteries of deficiency

lunch was a trip to the local grocery
bologna on a hard roll
lots of mustard
and a large Coke
sandwiched in between
more meetings
more people

as the day progressed
the pace would quicken
the streets would awaken
and begin the day's action
a constant stream of humanity
would come to the Church of the Master
some because they needed something
some just to be around
I stayed put
and it kept happening
phones ringing
people coming
people going
laughter and horseplay would fill the halls
the crescendo of activity
just kept increasing
till the whole place was bouncing to capacity

building structure
on the non-structure
few scheduled meetings
just endless non-scheduled ones
an admonition to study
a few minutes listening to a heart in pain
challenging a youngster suspected of being on drugs
encouraging a potential dropout
sharing some simple truth of God's love
comforting a lad on the death of his father
answering somebody's need for a little attention

permeating all my effort
was a desire
to share Christ

a simple recognition
that only God could meet the deepest human needs
a commitment
to identify with suffering
and struggle for human justice
not out of paternalism
or guilt
(although much was no doubt present)
but in quiet obedience to the command of Jesus
to love thy neighbor as thyself
and an honest recognition
of the difficulty of that assignment
without His strength
or even with it

then the evening streetwork tour began
up and down Eighth Avenue
seeing the crowd
saying hello
identifying old friends
meeting new ones
a floating presence
along an avenue of need

so much great counseling
can be done
through a ministry of presence
and involvement
when you are around all the time
many great opportunities just happen
too much social work
is done by appointment
sometimes you can't really help
by seeing someone
a week from Tuesday
at three o'clock
sometimes you just have to be there
to be effective

finally it was back to the apartment
fellows arriving
fellows leaving
a constant hoard of visitors
and some permanent guests
talking
laughing

studying
arguing
watching TV
constant surveillance for drugs
continuous motivation
in the direction of the possible
in the climate of the impossible

a tired leader
would meet his pillow each night
remembering the man
from Greek mythology
who rolled the stone up the big hill
only to have to do it again
tomorrow

Yakka Flats

27 SOME BORROWED PRESENTS

Every good and perfect gift is from above, coming down from
the Father. . . .

James 1:17

Christmas
is the most depressing time of the year
in a ghetto
it is as if all the feelings somehow surface
exploding to the top
erupting over the brim
draining out
uncensored
people seemed to get drunker
higher
more depressed

materialism
seemed to be put on blatant display
for the duration of the holidays
like affluence was showing off
challenging people to see who could buy the most
rubbing it in
exaggerating
the disparity between
those who have
and those who have not

each year
the Church of the Master
got a limited chance to play Santa Claus
stores and suburban churches
would throw stuff our way
off the top

the whole week before Christmas
the gifts kept coming
I put them all under lock and key
in the office

all the time
each of the fellows was wondering
how to get his share
or to be perfectly honest
how to get more than his share

I was inundated with kindness
friendliness
cooperation
sweet talk

on the day before Christmas
I called the fellows in
one at a time
a quiet encounter
some encouragement to go on
and a small pile of presents for each of them
to be distributed
to those they loved best

as the day progressed
the intensity of the emotional contact
of the ghetto at Christmas time
began to affect me
to cast a deadly pall over everything
the longer it lasted
the deeper the depression

I was virtually broke
and faced a Christmas of poverty
what little money I had saved
for some presents for my little kids
had long since been spent
on someone else's need

I passed out the presents
and with some troubling internal rationalization
I began to build a small pile for myself
topped off by the best doll in the place
for my little girl

I quietly put my gifts in my car
to head for home

to be a hero
I bought the Christmas tree
but the gifts were borrowed from the ghetto
and brought back to suburbia
on a special mission
of love and care

the little kids
never asked their daddy
where he had gotten the presents
little kids are that way

28   THE EMOTION OF ASHES

As he approached Jerusalem and saw the city, he wept over it
and said, "If you, even you had only known on this day what
would bring you peace. . . ."

Luke 19:41, 42

the apartments had secure walls
they afforded a refuge
a base
a home
but outside a storm was brewing

and one day Harlem exploded
the status ghetto of our land
began vomitting what it had swallowed for years
it was as if we all went temporarily insane
tanks and national guardsmen
patrolled the streets of great American cities
fear echoing fear
despair emulating despair
something was woefully amiss
the trouble was deeply rooted
within the social fabric
of a great nation
people violently protested
what a democracy had done with race
what freedom had done with color

I was on Eighth Avenue in Harlem
when the trouble broke
in a riot
absolutely anything can happen
and does

restraints are eliminated
a climate of absolute permissiveness is created
it's infectious
people get high on it
like all the boredom
and frustration
and defeat
and anger
had just piled up
and now it had exploded
irrationally
people were out of control

the disturbance was progressive
block after block
it was like a row of dominoes
topling in successive defeat
first the gates
then the sound of breaking glass
then the removal of the contents of the stores
then smoke
and then fire
then the spinning redness
of fire trucks
and police cars
which dispersed the crowd
only to have them repeat the process
on the next block

for several hours
I watched some strange happenings
there was constant suspense
total action
and massive destruction
it culminated in violent fire
casting the silhouette of a riot
into the black sky of the ghetto
madness was in the air
riveting the attention of the nation
upon the grievance of a people
like the thing had built up emotionally
collecting
contaminating
twisting
thwarting

oppressive weight
growing heavier
grinding
immobilizing
constantly reducing alternatives
until there were none
except
to explode
Harlem the symbol of black America
in a defiant gesture
was telling the whole world
that something was tragically wrong

an emotion of ashes
spread throughout America
deep expressions of guilt
and concern
what have we done
what can we do

America's leadership responded
with an attitude of "lets get moving"
we'll roll up our sleeves
and conquer this problem
the great society
escalated its war on poverty
the most powerful nation
in the history of the world
might have neglected its slums
but the problem would soon be corrected

our country might have won all its wars
and mastered most of its challenges
but the sixties presented us with two problems
we would not overcome
a war in Viet Nam
and a war within our cities
both were to drain our resources
and sorely trouble our conscience
but long after Viet Nam
has faded into a horrible memory
the urban problem will still haunt us
with no truce in sight
no peace at hand

29   A BORROWED SOLUTION

despite the riots
despite the destruction
the streets still held
an unlimited milieu for friendship
there was no legitimate competition
for concern

a program of friendship
was the great urban program
the ultimate program
that is what the battered streets
needed
wanted
and it so happened
that friendship
was exactly what the Christian faith
is supposed to be good at
Christ of the market place
the friend of publican and sinners

streetwork became
the driving force of the program
a person out of his own life
giving strength and meaning
to the lives of others
the streetworker was an agent of motivation
an interested adult
who would take the time and trouble
to be a friend of youth
he becomes a substitute
for a broken-down family structure
he becomes the great encourager

he talks
pleads
scolds
molds

I had come to know very well
so many young sons of the ghetto
but their lives
had so many problems
and problems must have
substantive answers
you can't make an urban friendship
and then send the youth to educational structures
that don't educate
to legal programs that don't defend
and so on
to get a quality job done
I came to find
we would have to develop our own structure

historically prep schools have been
educational oases for the privileged
we began to fashion
a very simple plan
to send some dropouts
we had befriended
to a prep school in Newark
an historic formula for the rich
being used for the poor
with great expectations

that first beautiful group of young men
who went to prep school
didn't happen by accident
it wasn't the effort of a truant officer
or the result of our ad in the paper
motivating dropouts
is not so much recruiting
as relating
more like what happens around a good home
than an Army induction center
whether they went back to school
mattered
was important
the fulcrum for much of the future
the difference between

little and more
a stock boy or a lawyer
the extent you could help your mother
your own children someday
in many cases the stakes were even higher
between being a junkie or not
being in jail or not
being alive or not

they soon came with their prep school report cards
official acknowledgment of academic progress
the results were breathtaking
they represented unusual achievement
compiled by a group of dropouts
straight off the streets
educational rejects
making it
I spread the report cards out in front of me
covering a table top with progress
it was an indictment
against the educational establishment
'put the system on trial
present the report cards as evidence
call them as the first witness
repent
somebody repent
these kids were destroyed
look at the prep school report cards
look at the records of resurrection
look *see* for yourself
what made these sons of the street
get such good marks
after long histories of educational failure
if these two dozen young men have done so well
let us find out why
and duplicate the answer
all over the public educational system'

Harlem didn't even have a high school
what pressures of planning
destroyed the blueprints
what insane edict
caused this miscarriage of construction
why was the educational womb
of a great community

barren all those years
our fellows were doing so well at Newark Prep
we began to have a great dream
why couldn't we begin a prep school in Harlem
a place where a little kid
bouncing a ball on dirty streets
could focus his daydreams
a place that would compete
with drugs
hustlers
broken dreams
crushed lives
and give witness
to an alternative
Harlem Prep could become
an example of quality education
which could speak to the nation
about what could happen
in every ghetto

the birth of Harlem Prep
became very important
and dominated lots of our efforts

30   THE STREET ACADEMY PROGRAM

The Urban League was unique among the civil rights groups that thrived in the sixties. Besides having a long tradition of activity in every major city, the League had racially integrated boards and a solid rapport with business and political leaders. The organization emphasized program, not protest. They specialized in revitalizing educational systems, addressing housing problems and creating job opportunities for the poor. For these reasons, the corporations and foundations who were now becoming involved in the ghetto found the League to be an attractive avenue for their outreach.

In June of 1966 Dr. Callender left the Church of the Master and became the executive director of the New York Urban League. He gave us an exciting base from which to expand our activities. I didn't have much stuff to move into my new office but I did have a program and because everybody at the Urban League wanted to know what it was called it seemed natural to say the Street Academy Program.

> it was not born of some great creative moment
> just sort of happened
> a logical extension
> of what we were thinking yesterday
> dropouts were making it at Newark Prep
> but they made it best
> when they went through
> a preparation experience
> why not extend the process
> to the street level
> put an educational unit
> right out there on the streets
> making it as accessible as possible
> it could be called a street academy
> creating the beginnings
> of an educational ladder

if the student did well
he would be sent to prep school
rewarding achievement
with rapid advancement
but also protecting development
from failure

we picked one of the worst corners in Harlem
for the first street academy
and dropped our anchor
Eighth Avenue and 114th Street
an unbelievable crossroad
of human decay
in the heart of the drug traffic
pulsating with so much
that was so wrong
it was a raggedy storefront
badly in need of repair
and renovations left much to be desired
but it became home
it was an incredible sight
to see how kids flocked to that storefront
there was no big sign
no fancy equipment
just some teachers and streetworkers
who cared about kids
it had a basic educational curriculum
and a message of hope

the educational leadership for the program
came from Dr. Susie Bryant
she had taught for a long time
in a black college down south
and had come north to retire
we hired her to work in the program
and from the beginning
she constantly stressed
"these youth do not need to be entertained
they need to know how to read and write
there are no magic curriculums
that will wipe out remedial deficiencies
it's the basics
stick to them Harv
stick to them"

a well run street academy class
sometimes resembled a university seminar
at other times the one-room school house
sometimes a group therapy session
perhaps at times
a regular high school classroom
and often just chaos

but programs are more than sound methods
they are implemented by staff
and we had a diverse group
of qualified people
Africans
and some folks with African names
people who had been to college
and some who had been to jail
staff who were serious
some who were learning to be
folks who lived in Harlem
some who just worked there
dedicated Christians
committed Muslims
and many who really didn't believe anything
white radicals
black militants
and most everything in between
they were all there
a divergent expression
about a common goal
of wanting to see some street kids
make it

the youth came to the street academy
responding to what they could see
attracted by what they could understand
new candidates
volunteering
because they wanted to try too
if these dudes can go to college
so can we
a little unrealistic you say
perhaps
but it was amazing
what aspiration could do to the human spirit

and how many of those street kids
ended up in college

Eighth Avenue was Harlem
some of the worst of it
pawn shops
liquor stores
junkies
cheap eating places
storefront churches
but no corporate presence
except a stray Coca Cola bottle cap
or a discarded cigarette package
no car dealerships
no major franchise stores
no visible evidence
of our nation's business strength
I had a sound idea
I wanted businesses to sponsor street academies
and put their names on them
to give visible evidence
of a commitment to do something
an attempt to bring
some of the greatest corporate names of America
to the streets of Harlem
to lend their identity
to a creative idea that works
I was determined that someday
you could walk down Eighth Avenue
and see the IBM street academy
the RCA street academy
the General Motors street academy
among the blighted remnants
of what was left

Harlem Prep finally became a reality
an abandoned supermarket
was purchased with foundation grants
Harlem now had its own prep school
and Eighth Avenue had a new symbol
to compete with all the rest
and now there was added incentive
to go to a street academy
work real hard
and you can go to Harlem Prep

the riots had produced
a great willingness to help
the corporate leaders of America
came up to Harlem to offer assistance
my visitors were unlimited
or only limited by my capacity
to receive them
I remembered once
when my mother went away for two weeks
and I was supposed to water the plants
but forgot
until the day before her return
I then gave them two weeks of water
all at once
but you can't water plants that way
the urban breakthroughs
were unbelievable
but I knew that before long
the focus of America's conscience
would find new directions
and I would soon be wishing
I could have some of those conversations
there wasn't time to have
but one thing was for sure
the corporations at this moment of time
were going to sponsor
all the street academies we wanted

despite the commitment
at times we still held our breath
one of the corporations
asked us to give one of their people
an orientation to the program
one night in one of the academies
as we were showing him around
there was a shattering of glass
and everyone hit the floor
someone had just fired a shot
and just missed the corporate man
a shot in the dark
which almost caused havoc
but our new friend never told
the corporate people downtown
about that part of the orientation

116

and donors remained reassured
that it was all right for them
to come to the ghetto

the pioneers used to park
their covered wagons in a circle
consolidating their resources
against the enemies of the night
I felt that circumstance
dictated the same bunching mentality
for the street academy program
IBM
Atlantic-Richfield
Celanese
Pan-Am
Time-Life
became neighbors
in a new kind of corporate park

it was an incredible thing
to begin to hear youth in Harlem say
"I'm going to school at IBM"
or "I'm going up to Time-Life"
or "meet you later at Pan-Am"

the Eighth Avenue cluster
became a concentration of activity
a place where a student
could bring any problem
banks have branches
airlines have travel agencies
corporations have salesmen
but the public educational response was centralization
the removal of all activities
into large impersonal units
located miles from the foci of action

the street academies
were like extended families
a serious effort to reproduce
the needed givens
the restoration of community
in the midst of the estranged
some corporations said
"here's the money go renovate your academy"

from others it was
"come let us do it together"
no corporation tried harder than Celanese
first it took forever
to get a building permit
then a local contractor
ran away with his advance money
but Celanese was still as cooperative
as they were patient
they got these great rugs
and some of the executives in the company
donated some weekend time
to clean out the back lot
which hadn't been done
since about the first world war
and that's a whole lot of wine bottles
then they came back some more
and planted some grass
and I think that they were even going
to build a patio in the spring
when tragedy struck again
one weekend the junkies broke in
and stole the rugs
two weekends later the junkies came again
this time they stole all the plumbing
including the toilet bowl
so we still didn't have a Celanese street academy
but in the ghetto to be successful
you just don't quit
you keep on going
despite
the whole new blanket of wine bottles
on the freshly planted sod
out back

there was plenty of trouble on Eighth Avenue
I was under one redundant pressure
"get all the white faces
off the Avenue"
there really weren't
that many of them
one was Felix
who had been with the program
since the beginning

he was a dedicated person
and a brilliant teacher
what was the sense
of discarding that kind of talent
I took a stand
Felix is not moving
"it's very confusing my man
no easy answers
or clear cut alternatives
whites and blacks
are going to remain confused
for a long time to come
and in the meantime
we're going to make some mistakes
about leaving and staying"

all in all
it was constant brinkmanship
each day raised the distinct threat
of producing the events
which would blow the project
into a whole lot of pieces
the levels of difficulty kept increasing
the militant pressure was draining
the task of developing a program
which depended so heavily
upon indigenous leadership
was awesome
most of the whites in the program
were very young
and often working on their first real job
the struggles were endless
absolutely endless
corrected today
only to become unglued
again and again
fatigue was fast closing in
the black-white tensions were relentless
the same meetings
over and over again
it was like squeezing air
from one part of an underinflated balloon
to another

but the students were doing so great
hundreds and hundreds of them now
were moving through the academies
on to prep school
and off to college

31   THE COOL BREEZE

the face was unique
etched in frozen hardness
you instinctively knew
that face had lived through the difficult
yet a strength prevailed amongst the features
reflecting the evidence of a fierce struggle
a refusal to capitulate
to the obvious
yet the scars of the effort
remained
so you could see
if you cared to
about what had happened to Aubrey Matthews

most people called him the "Cool Breeze"
don't know why
and we can't ask him anymore
because
one day he stopped living

no one could catch an attitude like Aubrey
in fact in some ways
Aubrey was one perpetual attitude
relating to the Cool Breeze was like cracking a code
deciphering hieroglyphics
yet there would be the sudden flash of kindness
the loud infectious laugh
the flow of humanity
that just made you like him

Aubrey wanted to go to prep school
with the rest of the fellows

but his head
wasn't fashioned for the task
he soon faded
like a cut flower
who wanted life
but had no roots

Aubrey joined a street academy
his response was a sacred testament
to the validity of the new school
the academy provided Aubrey
with an atmosphere in which to grow

I later hired Aubrey
to be the streetworker
at a street academy
the first alumnus to fill the position
and what amazing progress
penetrated Breeze's life
smiling toughness
up and down the streets
like a limited black Moses
a shepherd
rounding up his sheep
and heading them at least briefly
in the right direction
a product of the streets
now using what he knew best
to help others

my mother gave me a new coat for Christmas
it was sort of an annual thing
I never really liked to wear coats
my mother was always concerned that I did
this year's coat was very beautiful
and real warm
but it was cashmere
a little inappropriate
for the ghetto
so I decided to give it to Aubrey
and the big fellow loved it
the "Cool Breeze" on the streets of Harlem
in my cashmere
the coat was perhaps symbolic
I had shared

a lot of things with Aubrey Matthews
and there was
lots of exciting growth
to see for the exchange
yet sometimes
I would get flashes of doubt
about Aubrey's development
what had he made his own
and what was he wearing that belonged to others

drugs were now dominating Harlem
wasting so much in their path
Aubrey swallowed the contamination
inundated by his friends
and his own brokenness
a human being of great worth
was destroyed
so much promising potential
was annihilated

Aubrey died of a massive overdose of evil
ruptured by all that was wrong in the ghetto
like his body just got saturated
and sunk
they said he died of hepatitis
and pneumonia
and a few other things
but the complications could all be
traced to one curse
heroin

Aubrey had responded to Christ
and believed right
but died wrong
Aubrey a child of God
was overcome by drugs

Aubrey was an irreplaceable symbol to me
and when he died
something in me did too
like some incentive
had been ripped away
to me Aubrey never seemed slow
never seemed poor
never seemed damaged
he had somehow transcended all labels

in some beautiful way
he was just the "Cool Breeze"
period
and now
he was gone

"Cool Breeze"

32   IN THE TRENCHES

- it was a quiet day
at the street academy
the argument started
over a spilled soda bottle
an accidental incident
that led to words
because it was Cobra's elbow
and Turnip's lap
the two adversaries
hurriedly left the academy
to go home
to get their guns
a shootout at O.K. corral
ghetto style
on a crowded Harlem street
I stood between two men
who wanted to hurt each other
but I was also between two men
who wanted to back down
to save face
to express themselves with rhetoric
not guns
however life often is spent cheaply in the ghetto
people have died for lots of little things
a few dollars owed
an argument
mistaken identity
even over such small things
like spilled Coke

- what was becoming obvious
was that so many of the students

couldn't read
but how could a youth
make it to high school
and be reading
at a third and fourth grade level
some couldn't read at all
I knew that you couldn't
leave them in the first grade
for eight years
but there must be a better alternative
to sending them
from grade to grade
like an unopened letter

• Tony had a big mouth. He was always disturbing someone with his loud talk. Luther stuttered. He covered it up by being quiet. Both Tony and Luther were in my street academy.

One day the academy had become intolerable. Noise and confusion were everywhere. Tony was being his usual loud self. Finally I exploded. "Everyone shut up now! The next person who says anything has had it!"

My emotional outburst produced the desired results. Silence prevailed. I began to speak with deep concern.

"You've got to take a serious look at yourself. So many of you are doing so badly. If you drop out of here there is little hope left. For some of you this is your last chance. This is 'the last chance academy.' You've got to begin to care. Care for yourself. Care for your future. And you've got to care for each other. Help each other. Tony, you talk too much. Always bothering people with your big mouth. And Luther, you never talk and yet I know you've got so much to say. That is what our academy has got to become. A group of people who help each other. Luther you've got to help Tony to shut up and Tony you've got to help Luther to talk."

Everybody in the room was real quiet. A mood of subdued thought had fallen on a street academy.

• I am besieged.

"Harv, they haven't paid the bill yet."

"Harv, he's dead. He died of an overdose."

"My check is wrong. I've got to have a new one today."

"Harv, they said they wouldn't renew the contract."

"Harv, Bucky got mugged cutting through the park. He got stabbed and it looks bad. Get down to the hospital right away."

"Harv, the econoline won't start."

"I lost my job because I hit a fellow correction officer who stole something from my apartment. I need a job."

And I respond.

"Please send them the check. This is the second voucher I've signed. The people are entitled to their money."

"Why don't you have a staff meeting. It won't work without coordination. I'm just trying to be helpful but you can't run a good street academy without giving your people a chance to get together."

"Look, you can't do it that way. It just won't work. They won't fund it. Look, it ain't about your being black or them racist, you just can't do it that way."

"So what has that got to do with it. You can't be a streetworker without working at night."

"Bucky, you're fortunate. They had to remove your gallbladder but you will be all right."

"So your tooth hurts, but you can still make a special effort to come to work."

"Sounds great! You're doing a terrific job. Thanks for sharing it with me."

"Man don't scream at me. It's not my fault. What do you want me to do?"

                    the student appreciated
                    what Herman had done for him
                    and it really wasn't
                    all that much
                    just an adult
                    who spent some time caring
                    for someone who never had very much
                    because Herman had become
                    his great hero
                    the student took his savings
                    and bought two tickets
                    for a concert in the arena
                    he asked Herman to come with him
                    a big occasion
                    with his admired friend
                    Herman didn't mean to forget
                    but unfortunately he did
                    and the student was left
                    to go alone

128

except he didn't
he just sadly walked the streets
cursing the fate
of his former friend
as he ripped the tickets
into little shreds
leaving a trail of sorrow
Herman was crushed
by his incredible oversight
he kept asking the student
to forgive
what he had forgotten
but it was to no avail
there was no potential to do penance
for the next few weeks
everybody in the project got to hear
over and over again
about what Herman had forgotten

think of all the urban youth in America
who are so susceptible to genuine attention
and think of all the people
who are being paid
to give that attention
what would happen
if we did
think of all the opportunities
we are missing
and the frightful price we are paying
for our oversights

33　COMPLEX DIVISIONS

I went to the ghetto to share Christ. I soon found out that I had to share a lot of other things. In a suburban setting most of the physical needs of the teenager are met by the family. In an urban setting family structures are usually strained, broken or nonexistent. Urban kids are often years behind in school, have drug habits, cases in court, or have already fathered or mothered children. No ghetto ministry can be effective without addressing the physical needs of youth as well as those of a spiritual nature.

I had sought and received permission from Young Life to enter into an unorthodox dichotomy. In addition to remaining in charge of Young Life in the New York area, I had become the director of the Street Academy Program for the New York Urban League. My two jobs put sufficient resources under my jurisdiction to meet both the physcial and the spiritual needs of the youths we served. But my novel approach to urban ministry invited unsettling questions from both camps.

"Why does he get so involved in educational projects, in legal programs and who knows what else. Why doesn't he stick with spiritual programs?"

"Who does he work for? Who owns him?"

"Why is he bending Young Life out of shape?"

"It's a few white Young Life people who are making decisions for the Urban League in a back room somewhere."

The leadership of Young Life was almost entirely unfamiliar with the mandates of urban ministry. A lack of knowledge sometimes induces fear. It also produces a climate of criticism. I was an inexperienced manager directing a large program on chaotic streets. Critics could easily find many exposed targets at which to snipe—for whatever reason.

The Urban League had a set of concerns all their own. The League consisted of a staff of roughly fifty who were mostly middle-class blacks. Now suddenly they were joined by two hundred new recruits, many of whom were either street blacks or whites. Understandably, such diversity engendered pressures that were not readily assimilable. As the program grew we encountered further struggles over its resources. How much overhead should be charged for administration? Who had the power to hire new workers? How much control did Harv have?

Our program moved ahead under the power of its own imaginative appeal and the reborn emphasis on the ghetto ushered in by the riots. But even an uninitiated observer could ascertain that the seas ahead were stormy.

34 INVOLVED

The committee rooms and the streets shared little in common. The concerns of one were not the needs of the other. Matched against the pressures of the project, the concerns of the Urban League or Young Life leaders seemed too diminutive to worry about just then.

- it was hot
  humid hot
  and the kids were
  turning on the hydrants
  the example of one
  produced the example
  of another
  and another
  the momentum of the water
  gushing into forceful streams
  somehow seemed to
  reduce the pressure
  that a summer heat
  builds up
  in the ghetto

- the policeman crossed the street
  with a worried look on his face
  I was standing on a street corner
  surrounded by a half dozen blacks
  having a serious discussion
  about something or another
  I could understand
  the policeman's anxiety
  in Harlem you just don't see
  white guys and black guys

standing on a corner
enjoying a friendship

• the phone ripped into the silence of the night
Bob Summers had drowned in Africa
of all the things to go wrong
it seemed endless
pressures
obstacles
we put all kinds of effort
into sending some of our best students to Africa
and right in the middle of it
a kid drowns
part of the tragedy of Summers' death
is what had happened in his life
he had kicked a drug habit
and turned his whole life around
he was doing so well in prep school
headed for college
and he gets his life snatched from him
he had left one jungle
to die by the peaceful shores of another
we flew his body home
a sad mother
mourned the death
of her only son

• the rest of the students returned
from Africa
with tales
of their adventures
in the dark continent
travelling through Ghana
meeting with students in the Capecoast University
seeing the city of Accra
exploring crumbling ruins
of old and ancient civilizations
which have succumbed to time
Nigeria
Nairobi
Kenya
Tanzania
living for week long periods
with families
in village settlements

Masailand
Serengetti Plains
Ngarongaro Crater
Kilimanjaro
Mombasa and Dar es Salaam
and the Ilse of Lamu
the wellspring of Swahili poetry
a streetworker said
that the most revealing experience of the trip
was walking through an African city
the American students
with their Afros
and dashiki
among Africans
wearing western clothes
and blond wigs
a contemporary cultural exchange
was playing some mean tricks
on who was copying whom

- One day a black advertising man came into the office with an idea. He wanted to promote a football game in New York between two black colleges for the benefit of the Street Academy Program. He said he could get Morgan State and Grambling to play the game. Most everyone thought the idea was insane. Even Notre Dame could no longer draw a crowd in Yankee Stadium. The man said that if we filled all the seats, the program could raise over two hundred thousand dollars. And so it was arranged—a football game in Yankee Stadium between Morgan State and Grambling.

  We sold out Yankee Stadium several days before the game. You couldn't get a ticket. The audience was mostly black and largely from the streets. Talk about the game had circulated for weeks in the bars and corners of the ghettos. Advertisements had been posted on every pole and broken parking meter in Harlem. For years blacks had watched white teams play in New York. Now they had a chance to see their own with all the props of the big time. The game took on the atmosphere of a carnival—a giant social event in the black community.

  The police were out in force as if they feared a riot would break out if sixty thousand black people ever assembled in one place. But there wasn't even the semblance of trouble. And why should there have been? It was one of the few times when whoever won was black.

- Of the principals who emerged to lead the black cause in the sixties, one of the strongest was Malcolm X. After his tragic death, I hired

134

many of his staff to work on the program. I was attracted to their manhood and spiritual interest. They hated poverty pimps, black preachers, black politicians, and talked endlessly about middle-class negroes and self-appointed leaders of the poor. The black man's survival must be rooted in himself and his African past, they maintained.

Malcolm's men also gave me lots of lectures on economics. Whitey had fiscal control of Harlem. The poverty dollar only bounced once in Harlem so when the black man spent it, it went to something he didn't own and immediately left the community. The only answer was for blacks to control their own economic destiny.

And they talked about strength. I was repeatedly impressed with their courage. One of them told me, "With Rap Brown or Carmichael, you had to be violent. With Martin Luther King you had to be nonviolent. With Malcolm you could be everything. He was the cleanest image of a man." My Muslim friends were determined to crush the black matriarchal structure. The black man needed to be strong so that he could lead his community. I owed a great debt to their wisdom. They were men. They were black men. And they had compassion for their people.

- I circled the block
  with a face that looked like death
  I did not want to go
  into that building
  I did not want
  to ask another person for money
  the emotional pressure
  that bears down upon you
  yet you must keep your composure
  you must ask
  with a little defiance
  the sacred task of translation
  of convincing someone
  that the needs of the ghetto
  must be responded to
  a task so hard
  it goes against human nature
  ties your insides into a knot
  fills you with fear
  you think of all the reasons
  to run away
  to quit
  I can't go in there

I don't want to
I can't
that kind of pressure
tears you awake in the morning
with an emotional threat
hanging over your life
today you must ask for money
at stake was vital creativity
or some essential human need
which would again
be dashed into a thousand pieces
unless the fiscal substance
could be found

• In 1968 Dr. John Coburn resigned as dean of the Episcopal Theological School in Boston to teach English in a Harlem Street Academy. He stated the reason for his move as "a desire to practice what I preach." Dean Coburn said, "Along with social changes, the Church may help provide educational changes and undergird both with a reminder that all change is the attempt to help change men's hearts so that reconciliation may be effective person to person, race to race and generation to generation." I wish every religious leader in America could follow Dr. Coburn's meaningful example and spend a year on the streets with the poor. He is now the Bishop of Massachusetts.

• they called themselves "urban deadline"
expressions of the counter-culture
graduates or dropouts
from the best colleges in the country
who refused to join the status quo
and had come to Harlem instead
to help to rebuild the ghetto
dropouts from the establishment
helping to build storefronts
to prepare youth from the streets
to go to the same colleges and graduate schools
some of them had dropped out from
the times had produced
some strange irony
from the homes of the affluent
working with the poor
brilliant minds
laboring with their hands
products of contemporary affluence
trying to find meaning

136

questioning the whole premise of their preparation
with some profound gesture
of defiance
and quest

• We were in the Roosevelt Room of the White House. Some of the top social and educational leadership of the administration were there. There was a long discussion about the poor. We had some answers but the response to suggestions of national replication was that it was impractical. One of the cabinet members said that the federal government is like an elephant and you can't make an elephant walk through tulips. One of us offered to become an elephant trainer and the meeting got a little heated. The next day I was in Harlem and I had an insight as I looked at all the poor people on the street and reflected on yesterday's White House meeting. The issue wasn't about elephants walking through tulips like the Secretary had suggested. It was about the elephant walking over people and somehow we ought to find ways to train him.

• I was sitting in the back of a limousine showing the President's wife the poor sections of the ghetto. I was going to say escorting her, but that would not have been true. The secret service were the escorts. They had also done a thorough job in preparation for her tour. Major expressways had been cleared of all traffic. The route was meticulously planned. The surveillance was complete. What if the government could structure urban social programs with the same care? We would give the poor some whole new directions and some unusual social security.

• I stood in the back of the room watching a young leader attempting to communicate the nature of worship to sixty Harlem teenagers. He told them that worship not only had something to do with man and God but also with each other. Worship begins with the community that loves each other.

The leader told them there would be a three-minute worship service consisting of looking around the room seeing who God wanted them to love. There was some embarrassment and a few giggles. Willie saw a roach climbing up the back of "Onion's" jacket. He laughed loudly but then moved his chair so he could be serious. A room full of faces looked at who they could love.

It is hard to love what you can't see. It is difficult to respond to what you don't know about.

There are many people in our country who would respond to the plight of the ghetto if they were only exposed to it. It is hard to have conviction without participation.

35 OVERWHELMED

Save me, O God,
for the waters have come up to my neck,
I sink in the miry depths,
where there is no foothold. . . .
I am worn out calling for help;
my throat is parched.
My eyes fail,
looking for my God.
Those who hate me without reason
outnumber the hairs of my head;
many are my enemies without cause. . . .

Ps. 69:1-4

One night I was working late. My Harlem office was suddenly invaded by a dozen or so black men. They surrounded me and began to do their menacing thing. They demanded that I stop teaching their children and told me to leave the community forever. If I did not comply, they would enforce their edict with violence.

The invading so-called militants used tactics that I would soon become very familiar with. They usually traveled in large packs, stalking their prey much like the KKK. They seemed to need the security of numbers to express their courage.

I didn't need to demonstrate my courage. My daily presence in Harlem testified to that. When confronted on that evening I did the only thing I felt I could do. I put my hands behind my back, hung my head, avoided all eye contact and quietly stood there. I had no defense.

While I deplored the methods of the invaders, I understood their concern. They were addressing themselves to the intensely sensitive issue of white presence in a black community. I used to debate the issue constantly with myself. "Should I be leading a large project in Harlem?" Most days I

138

desperately wanted to leave. Not just because I was white, but because the task was too impossible. I stayed only because of one reason—my faith.

But the confrontations came almost daily and pointed to the need for a defense. My size would often work against me. At 6-2 and 220 I appeared an acceptable challenge. Sometimes my antagonists would come eyeball to eyeball with me, hoping to provoke a situation to test my courage.

A fellow streetworker confided to me that Harlem demands that one use violence or the threat of violence to maintain one's integrity. I toyed with the idea of defending myself with karate, and even took a few lessons. But I abandoned the effort quickly. Kung Fu might work on TV but it just couldn't be my strategy in the ghetto. I felt my only chance was to use my wits, finesse, courage, diplomacy, love, and leverage to somehow survive. And some days that didn't seem as if it would be for very long.

There were so many days when the project seemed out of control and threatened at any time to be dashed into a thousand pieces. But I had seen that many times now. I knew from experience that no matter how hopeless it looked, the ship somehow managed to stay afloat—at least long enough to face the next series of menacing waves. It was like walking through glass on bare feet: every issue became a potential sharp confrontation. Like the psalmist, I was being "chased by a lion only to be met by a bear."

But I couldn't stop the confrontations. And I couldn't back down. So I was forced into a room with a cheering section already there as they barricaded the door. Sometimes I would be challenged with loaded guns or open knives. Or the ash tray would be tossed inaccurately at my head and shatter into a thousand pieces against the radiator. I would constantly be challenged by people stronger than me.

Often I would get completely exasperated. Why was I the target of so much energy when there was so much around me which desperately needed attention? If they could have spent the time planning some constructive action instead of plotting against me, a good many poor people could have been helped.

Some street folk insisted: "Harv, we need you. Without you it would all fall apart." But still others shouted: "Get your white rear end out of here right away. You deliberately didn't train us. You wanted to create dependency, the old historic game you run on the black community. You made yourself irreplaceable running your academies like your white ancestors ran their plantations, telling your niggers what to do next because only you can get to the resources and only you know how it all works."

There were a few who wanted me to stay just to raise money, giving up my position. Some pressed me to go saying: "Leave, they will bleed you to death. You've done all you can or should."

In weariness I struggled on. My internal dialogue continued: "Why not just leave? Walk away and say 'I did what I could.' I can't go on working in the middle of this animosity and confusion." But I couldn't give up. I would have had to desert people I cared for and to abandon things I had worked so hard to accomplish.

The accusations and threats continued relentlessly. I was a vulnerable white man up for grabs attempting to survive. And I was so tired, so very tired.

36 DEADLINES OF THE MAJORITY

My enemies shout against me and threaten me with death.
They surround me with terror and plot to kill me. Their fury
and hatred rise to engulf me.

Ps. 55:3

one day they handed me
another deadline
"get out of Harlem
and you've got till groundhog's day
or else you die
remember now
you've got till groundhog's day"

all my life
I had thought about
how white folks
mistreated black folks
but I now knew why

the problem isn't just about white folks and black folks
its about human nature
because if all the white folks were black
and all the black folks were white
then some of the most
would pick on the least

I tried not to think about groundhog's day
they had sure picked an ignominious animal
on whose day I was to die
I wasn't even sure when groundhog's day was
or why it was significant
I thought it had something to do
with shadows

O God, have pity, for I am trusting you! I will hide beneath the
shadow of your wings until the storm is past.

Ps. 57:1

37 BLINDSIDED

My "two-hatted" responsibilities produced many tensions. When Dr. Callender left the Urban League to work for the Mayor there were leadership changes at the League. People who were unfamiliar with the program were thrust into positions of critical authority. The program became so susceptible to in-fighting that much time and energy was wasted in senseless struggle. There were other problems too. The money from the football game never arrived. The directors of Harlem Prep wanted to be independent from the Street Academy Program so that they would not have to restrict their enrollment to academy students. Renovations of all the storefronts were time consuming and the program looked like a construction company some days. As the project grew I found that I didn't know many of the students anymore. Most of the fellows with whom I had worked were now off in college and I didn't have the grass roots control that I once had. Finally, the national Urban League wanted to expand the program throughout the country and we were besieged by people from other cities who sought counsel.

As if the front office wasn't enough, I still had to deal with the streets. Someone was always creating some noise somewhere: a favor, a complaint, an emergency request. Drugs were a nightmare. The academies were perfect havens for their use and sale. We were always worried about potential staff involvement in the illegal activities—concerns which experience had proven to be relevant. But drugs weren't my only preoccupation. So many of the workers wanted pay raises, loans, special favors or my job.

Furthermore, the racial question was ever-present. The whiteness of myself and certain of our staff was a soft underbelly in the program. Anyone with an axe to grind could fan Whitey's dominance into an essential issue. A select group of people made it their business to cause disruption. The threat of violence was behind every door we opened and on every street we walked.

Still, I felt that I could outlast the racial and political pressure. I had extensive resources: a vital program, lots of friends, some loyal staff, and a spiritual commitment. My Young Life base was the cornerstone of my fortunes for it was the essential part of my spiritual and fiscal strength. But my urban translation of the gospel was creating organizational problems for them as well. I was leading Young Life into uncharted waters. Our lines of communication were increasingly littered with misunderstandings. I was being stretched and I figured Young Life could be too. However, I was wrong. One day without warning their leadership decided to terminate our relationship. Young Life cut me loose.

38   DIVISIONS IN THE BODY

no fracture
is as shearing
as a religious one
maybe because convictions run deeper
or expectations run higher
or something

"Why do you get so involved in secular projects?"

"I feel deeply about
the futility of preaching to a man's soul
and not taking care of his physical needs
the issues were germane
do it
or become ineffective
can you really preach to someone's heart
and not attempt to take care of the rest of his needs
I know that no vital faith
could be divided between secular and spiritual
the God of creation is inclusive
his dominance encompasses everything
there is nothing outside
the limit of his interest"

"Does vital faith have application to institutions?"

"part of the Christian faith
applies to bad schools
corrupt cops
decadent jails
ineffective courts"

the letter
was a dismissal

it came without warning
the crashing of a violent wave
a cruel and unwelcomed blow
that smashed me to bits
here
ultimate
involvement
in a huge ghetto
battling daily
against insurmountable odds
there
talk of separation
and division
and withdrawal of support
the event was jugular
the conditions so far-reaching
that protest was devoured by silence
and internal anguish remained unexpressed
but immediately
the bitter collection of resentment
began to assemble
and the saga of the abandoned began
on its lonely pilgrimage
towards destruction

manhood
courage
to shoulder the odds
unflinching
I had faced the wrath of Harlem
only to get beat by a roomful of white men
it was like I had caught the ghetto
swallowed too much of it
it had contaminated me
I was quarantined
turned me against the rest
put me on the wrong side of the ledger
the count was out of order
due process was distorted

I read it
with stunned disbelief
each word a betrayal
of all I believed sacred
it was wrong

inaccurate
an unholy indictment
of a servant of Christ
a heretical communication
how could he say what he said
it was wrong
insane
what utter misunderstanding of the issues
what cruel miscasting of the facts
come smell the urine in the elevator
watch the junkies die
live in the filth
see all the little kids distorted for life
walk the halls of educational disgrace
see the mutilation of justice
hear the hearts cry out
and the ones who should
but no longer do
because they can't
silenced
by neglect
and pain
hardening of the soul
immuned to help
and no longer capable
of salvation
and you say that I no longer fit the definition
well what is the definition
does it stop with niggers
and filth
and decay
and you say the reason I got kicked out
was because I didn't speak
the truth concerning life in our Lord Jesus Christ
madness
lies
lies
I spoke with tears in my eyes
I spoke with guns in my face
I cried out overwhelmed by all that I saw
I cried out for God
and to Him
were you there day after day as I walked those streets
do you know the brokenness I addressed

the long hours I tried
you say I didn't preach about Christ
I did
I did
oh God I did
I did till I was broken
broken
I've got nothing left to give
my speech runs dry
and you accuse me of not speaking
and you say
I am at the edge
of the furtherest frontier of social issues in our time
and then you leave me here to die
how can you say what you say

I cried out to my God
incapable of understanding
what was happening
I was as lost
as the streets
I had come to save

39   PAIN

I cried out to God for help; I cried out to God to hear me. When
I was in distress, I sought the Lord; at night I stretched out
untiring hands and my soul refused to be comforted.

Ps. 77:1, 2

pain
pain
it will not go away
it can't go away
it must work its way out
trapped in the small corners of the soul
like an emotional grinder
extracting its price
pain

betrayed
left alone
misunderstood
but alone
alone in pain
incapable of sharing it with anyone
because it wasn't meant to be shared
only endured
because that's what pain is
locked up hurt
you can't free
from the thing that produced it
in the first place

lost
lost in pain

lost like any lostness
you don't know where it ends
only what causes it
and it won't go away
because it can't
it clutches your insides
strangles you with wrong feelings
pulling
ruthlessly pulling
pain demands its results
like a determined shylock
that will not give up

stop
no more
but the cries of the heart
go unanswered

I knew more about the ghetto
than most white folks
and more about white people
than most black folks
that kind of knowledge
was too painful

40   AFTER SHOCK

O God, listen to me! Hear my prayer! For wherever I am . . . I will cry to you for help. When my heart is faint and overwhelmed, lead me to the mighty, towering rock of safety. For you are my refuge, a high tower where my enemies can never reach me.

Ps. 61:1-3

- he was very high
  and very depressed
  he had his gun out
  and sat there staring at me
  talking about wasting people
  I didn't know him well
  but he needed an audience
  "this whole thing you can't get your hands on
  this nebulous something
  always grappling at your neck
  holding you down
  the devil
  the evil
  man it's all over the place
  the thing that has destroyed
  our being
  our lives
  white man we hate you
  hate you
  hate you
  you have torn our manhood from us
  and debased our self-esteem
  but we can scream
  yell

carry on
white man we hate you"

• the meeting was an exercise in shouting
and threats
I sat there painfully
head bowed
refusing eye contact
why not spend the time
exploring new avenues of funding
or developing new creative ideas
or confronting the mafia about drugs
did it make any sense
to expose me
to all this irrelevance
I had made mistakes sure
there was room for improvement yes
but to subject me to all this vindictiveness
was the last thing I needed
I sat there for several hours
suffering through a sad charade
and as I sat there
I just gave up
I died
rigor mortis began to invade my exhausted insides
finally I excused myself
under the guise of some kind of emergency
and limped out of the room
to find some place to finish dying

• one of the academy teachers
was a very gifted black woman
but there was a personality clash
and her director wanted her fired
it became a terrible mess
and my responsibility to clean up

one day we had a long meeting
and I tried to resolve things
suddenly she angrily got up
called me a bad name
slapped me across the face
and stormed out of the room

I had been hit before
and harder

but somehow this was the blow
that shattered me
completely

who started this whole color thing anyway
it was sheer madness
categorical insanity
I had been forced by circumstances
to see too much
no longer could I hide my head in the sand
living with what wasn't
my innocence had been violated
I had looked in the mirror
and was seeing it straight
without censorship
most of the myths had been shattered
left was only the awful truth
the ghetto was a contradiction
of all I held precious
it violated my manhood
it adulterated my Christianity
it debased my whiteness
it wasn't vital democracy
it made a cruel mockery of freedom

for so many long years
I had personally participated
on the streets of a huge ghetto
every aspect of my life
had been affected by the experience
I could never return
to life as usual
but I was caught between two worlds
accused by one of being too much about blackness
accused by the other of being too much about whiteness
one I wanted to bring to the black streets
the other I wanted to bring into white institutions
where did I belong anyway
in bending myself to fit two worlds
I broke myself in half
and now I was out there
frantically looking for the pieces
I had seen too much of the ghetto
inhaled too deeply its awesome secrets
vivid impressions of cruel facts

had been seared into my brain
such knowledge demanded
some kind of ultimate response
and such commitment
I was more than willing to give
but I had to seek new forms of expression
I didn't know for sure what they were
but I did know a few places
not to bother looking anymore

41   THE CLOSE OF A CHAPTER

I resigned from the Street Academy Program. After the Young Life separation, my instincts told me to move on. For years and years I had been continuously on the streets. I was completely fatigued and needed a rest stop. No more meetings. No more hustling. No more rhetoric. No more for now.

The Program soon fell apart, partially because I left, but partially because the times had changed. Ghetto involvement was no longer "the thing to do," and the attentions of the corporations drifted elsewhere.

> I was sadly walking through Harlem
> it was a beautiful spring day
> everybody was out
> I sat down on a stoop
> for some rest and observation
> I began to reflect
> on all the hard work
> that had gone into the projects
> what once had been so strong and vital
> was now shattered into a thousand pieces
> I put my head in my hands
> and sobbed uncontrollably
> a deep expression of my grief
> a broken down junkie
> was about to sit next to me
> and ask what was wrong
> but thought better of it
> and moved away
> leaving the whole stoop
> to a broken down white man
>
> I would often begin to cry
> I didn't remember crying

my whole adult life
but now I cried quite often
like an overheating car radiator
boiling angrily to the surface

finding funding and people
to start all over again
was difficult business
somedays I felt like a pregnant elephant
waddling on
but I still believed
it could be done
and I believed that
because I knew it had to be done
and I knew that
because I had been to the ghetto

I was very tired
when I caught the cab
as the driver waited
for a light to change
he turned to me
and verbailzed
what he had been thinking
"this used to be
a fine section
houses were kept up
flowers grew in the yards
then the coloreds moved in
why can't they keep their houses up"
I was quiet for a moment
and was about to begin my cross-examination
when the light changed

for many long years
I had struggled my way
through the ghettos
but my efforts
were accompanied
by a whole lot
of psychic energy
everytime I walked down a street
my peripheral vision was out
ready to detect
unwelcome intrusions

a thrown missile
an unprovoked altercation
then the psychological pressures
that accompanied everything
each conversation
each meeting
had the potential for racial overtones
and sometimes confrontations
then there was the paranoia
of the unexpected
the fear of uncertainty
my black friends
just had no idea
of the vast amount of emotional energy
it took me
to work my way through a day

after I left Harlem
it was hard to relax
I kept hearing footsteps in the street
and voices in the dark
"relax Harv
relax
you are no longer in Harlem"
but Harlem was still in me
and would be
for a long time to come

I had a close friend
who had been to Viet Nam
he offered me
this probing insight
in Viet Nam
you never saw the enemy
differences were expressed
in the anonymity of gun fire
but in the ghetto
the confrontation was personal
you saw the hate
and the frustration
and had to participate
amidst its frightening velocity

all summer long
I travelled between my contrast
the consistency of suburbia

seemed as well guarded
as the chaos of Harlem
like walls had been constructed
that would never be breached
and neither side would really ever ask why
because each knew
I knew what my problem was
I now belonged to each
and the result was unsettled pain
like the pieces of my insides no longer fit together
and from the wound
of my incompatibility
bled questions
it was as if I had walked barefooted for too long
amid the glass of the ghetto
and even all the soft grass of suburbia
would not make the hurt go away

42   A DIFFICULT TRANSITION

the difficulty of seeing
the awful plight of the oppressed
the painful identity with a cause
embraced as truth
the futility of action
against hopeless odds
yet the necessity
to do something
the curse of knowledge
of not being able to forget
what you just keep remembering

from the first shattering moment
that I somewhat understood Harlem's plight
its trapped ugliness
its sad countenance
reflected so tragically
off the cement of a thousand abandoned streets
and lives
I felt the gospel and the ghetto
were a contradiction
that both could not exist
and there still be truth
my first efforts were so imperfect
but were filled with sincerity
and much youth and energy
I am so much wiser now
but the years have worn me down
my weariness and experience
now compete for dominance
and despite my intentions

I walk as a tree
sagging under a heavy burden of ice
I plead with you my Christian brothers
that we move out as we can
the rotten corruption of the streets
forms such an ungodly stench
that our spiritual community just must respond
people are helplessly trapped
in a chasm of such huge dimensions
that it just must appeal to our sense of justice
we have answers
we know truth
we have resources
perhaps some of us
can be some kind of burning bush
attracting the attention of a complacent church
to an unfinished task

the alarm clock pierced the light of dawn
with a sudden announcement
that day had come
I was so thankful
for my timely return to reality
I had been awakened from a massive nightmare
one of my ghetto enemies
was sitting in a hidden corner
waiting to kill me
one of my business friends
was recovering from a heart attack
but he ran away when he saw me coming
because he just didn't want to get involved
in any more projects
there was great difficulty
on a bus trip we had organized
and all the checks had gotten lost in the luggage
and people were getting paid
without working for it
I was saved by the alarm clock
but I woke up
with the same kind of depression I got
when things really went wrong
in the ghetto

throughout my ghetto struggles
I gained new insight

about the capacity of the human spirit
to erode under hardship
there are no strong and weak
it all depends
on the extent
of the pressure
every human being has a breaking point
there are no exceptions

my morale and spirit
were beginning to come back
there were plenty of relapses
but more and more recall
of the pre-ghetto years
and a growing capacity
to integrate the experience
into the total fabric of my life

I was not without my bad moments
times when depression
would strike like a summer storm
blotting out all traces of sun
and covering all in the path
with sudden fury
but there was progress
a healing
process
more smiles
less tears
and for that
I was thankful

but I had so much unfinished business
that great cluster of information
that I had collected
wisdom about the ghetto
that demanded expression
especially now that I was healing
my confidence was returning
my death wish ebbing
with the return of strength
came the renewal of vision
but dangers lurked
some loud voices
still echoed from the past

a slight flinch
still accompanied
the ringing of a telephone
recalling the memories
of power plays
fund raising deadlines
threats of physical violence
controversy
but I had made it
through the ghetto
I wanted to live again
to do something
about some things
I knew to be so wrong
I didn't cry anymore
but I never wanted to forget
what made me cry
yet there comes a time
when sorrow is no longer sorrow
the soul exhausts itself
and can no longer cry

reading and rereading the Scriptures
had a profound impact on me
"the prophets were the voice of God outraged
the voice of the poor violated"
deep within me
I wanted to be such a spirit

He gives strength to the weary
and increases the power of the weak . . .
But those who hope in the Lord
will renew their strength.
They will soar on wings like eagles;
they will run and not grow weary,
they will walk and not be faint.

Isa. 40:29-31

43 STRENGTH FOR TOMORROW

"Glory to God in the highest heaven," they sang, "and peace on earth for all those pleasing him."

Luke 2:14

it wasn't working out right
my car was parked at Newark airport
the only flights I could get from Orlando
landed at LaGuardia
that meant two long bus rides
in New York's Friday afternoon traffic
to get me to the right airport

the Florida sunshine
gave way to a New York December storm
the breath of winter beat against me
as I leaned against the driving rain
in search of my car
parked somewhere in the snowbanked lot

I was filled with depression
I was tired from a long week of travel
tired as only travel can make you
and then my car wouldn't start

I made my way
back through the chill
to the airport terminal
to call for help

Newark needs lots of things
an airport was one of them
the new one wasn't ready yet
the old one was a study in inadequacy

the entrance was crowded
with cars trying to unload passengers
close enough to keep them dry
and police frantically trying to unsnarl the process
one lady was blocking the door
because she was trying to open her umbrella
with two bags of oranges in her arms
she wasn't about to give up
on either the oranges or the umbrella
and all she was accomplishing
was hindering everyone else
from using the strategic spot
she was occupying

the terminal was crowded
on this Friday before the Friday before Christmas
businessmen and college students
all competed for space
on cancelled flights
impatient passengers
passing the time of delay
in search of distractions
doing a crossword
staring blankly into space
rereading the sports pages

I made my way
to a phone booth
suddenly the air was filled
with the beautiful sounds of the Hallelujah Chorus
a high school choir was singing
as choirs do
in public places
at Christmas time

a crowd of weary travelers
ringed the singers
in subdued silence
listening to the inspired music

I leaned on the side of a phone booth
and listened

in the midst of a crowded airport
at the height of confusion
to the backdrop of public address pronouncements
the kids sang their majestic song

Lord of Lords
King of Kings
forever and ever
the Lord shall reign forever and ever

in the midst of cancellation
the words of forever and ever
in the midst of tired humanity
the King of Kings
in the midst of the most mundane
a message of uniqueness

the incarnation
in a crowded Newark airport

I quietly thanked God
for the meaning of the event
and slowly turned to renew the struggle

44   RELUCTANCE

I called for a ride home from the airport that night. When it arrived I didn't hesitate, for I knew which way was home. The message of the airport was harder to discern. A part of me wanted to retire forever from the ghetto. Another part of me wanted to try some more. The final decision was a very difficult one.

the agony
of moving against the odds
of doing
what can't be done
of being so far out front
that it borders on irresponsibility
of being so possessed by an idea
that it captures you
devours you
threatens to render you ineffective

yet of such cloth
history is made
seas have parted
walls have crumbled
mountains have moved
but the bottom line
extracts its price
and the demanding question
must be asked
is it worth it

what about the others
those trapped in the wake
of the progress of an idea
family
friends
foes

those not privy to answers
only questions
those who saw not results
only what had been extracted
those left to feel cheated
forgotten
overlooked
abandoned
when is a cross
a cross
when is it an act of foolishness

when is what's right
wrong

when is faith
faith

when is faith
foolishness

and what roles do demons play
was Job unique on the stage of unreason
or are many more of us
unwitting victims
of spiritual conflicts
in high places

when are words enough
please
no more words

rest wants the weary
effort wants release
peace wants an opportunity
no more
cries the heart
come Christ
and let me enter into your rest
let me know your peace
may I express your love
may I know your plan
protect those I love
those for whom I couldn't do
what I hope to do

lead me on oh God
for that purpose
was I made

45 A DECADE OF DISCOVERY

I spent the decade which followed doing lots of things yet doing one thing: I was learning how to bring changes to the institutions that help the poor.

First I helped the United States Postal Service create a program for dropouts which was called Postal Academies. The Postmaster himself took the idea to the White House and within a few days he had executive approval, several million dollars and a scheduled press conference. It was another example to me of what influential people can do to help the poor. For the rest of the seventies, I developed a small organization that worked in various cities helping to create more efficient delivery of services to the poor through better coordination of existing resources.

Throughout the seventies I was intensely involved with institutional systems—the boards that controlled them, the supervisors who led them, the staff who ran them, the janitors who cleaned them and the clients they served. I worked with the poor and the powerful, with the managers and the managed, with those who had and those who wanted. I encountered bureaucrats who protected their turf and children who didn't have the skills to trespass on it. I also met many people in the system who struggled for change: dedicated principals, teachers, social workers, mayors, community workers. But the few were against the many. They were the ones who cared, who cried, who battled, but they were hopelessly outnumbered.

It was a decade of conflict. Tensions inherently pervade systems that deliver services to the poor. Insecurities, political survival, racial animosities, greed, need, fear, selfishness, depression, personality differences and so much else sweep through these structures often bringing out the worst in people. It was easy to get caught up in the conflicts. Attempting to change institutions invited additional conflicts; it was built into the system.

It was a decade of damaged children. Some couldn't read, others were caught up in drugs. Some faced the future unprepared and unskilled. Many had no fathers. Still more had no hope. Some were in jail or on the way there. The pregnant ones, the addicted ones, the unwanted ones, the confused ones—all were looking for answers that the institutions could not consistantly provide.

It was a decade of grants—the ones that came late, the ones that came flawed, the ones that never came at all. Some restricted our clients, some our staff, and some were so restricted as to be rendered useless. Most grants are obtained because of who you know. The worth of the cause or the quality of the program has little to do with the final decision.

It was a decade of decay. The creative energies of the sixties had dissipated. Housing stock had eroded to an alarming degree and abandoned buildings became the new symbol of the ghetto. The welfare system induced dependency. School systems were plagued by absenteeism and apathy. Drug dealers riveted themselves to street corners. The "joint" became what happened before school, during school and after school. The ghetto population exploded with children's children.

It was a decade of escalating costs. Welfare, food stamps and medicaid recipients proliferated, adding billions to the cost of maintaining poverty. Administrative expenditures correspondingly skyrocketed. The costs of American poverty were becoming unmanageable and impossible to fiscally sustain.

I participated in these years by running programs, evaluating projects, spending days in the halls of power and on the streets of the ghetto. I helped educators, politicians, community leaders and junkies. I contended with resistant bureaucrats, encouraged tired public servants and tried to piece together some coordinated resource for broken youth. I did lots of little things and some big things. Some days I was discouraged, others hopeful. The bottom line was that I was becoming very experienced. After almost three decades I had become wiser: fewer confrontations, greater understanding, less false starts, better management. Out of it all a plan was beginning to emerge that could begin to change urban America.

The decade of the seventies also left me with a disturbing observation: the Church of Jesus Christ had little urban presence. It was not a significant force in bringing change to the ghetto.

46   GOD'S WORKMANSHIP

I was sitting in a chair at the Mt. Zion Missionary Baptist Church in Los Angeles waiting to see Dr. E.V. Hill. I felt someone staring at me and looked up to see a beautiful black woman. I met her gaze and started to smile. I recognized her immediately.

I hadn't seen her for over a decade. Not since that day in Harlem when she had stormed out of the office after slapping me. She appeared so different and peaceful. She actually looked younger than she did ten years ago. Gone was the hardness that had characterized her.

She had become a Christian and Christ had changed her life. We had a deep talk about the spiritual changes in her life. Before I left she kissed my cheek in the same place she had hit me ten years before.

47 IN THE FULLNESS OF TIME

When you see the ark of the covenant of the Lord your God, and
the priests who are Levites, carrying it, you are to move out from
your positions and follow it. Then you will know which way to
go, since you have never been this way before.

Then Joshua told the people, "Consecrate yourselves, for tomorrow the Lord will do amazing things among you."

Josh. 3:3, 5

Following God is always unknown business. Abraham left on his pilgrimage not knowing the direction of his journey. Each true follower of God
emulates his example.

Two years ago my son, Timmy, became ill at college. Like so many students
he put off going to the clinic to receive care and a cold developed into
pneumonia. The nurse interviewed him as she filled out her routine form.
Name of father—Timmy could handle that. Father's occupation—Timmy
froze. Basically, he knew what I did but couldn't put it into an occupational
term. I understood Timmy's feelings. I was forty-seven, yet I still wondered
what I was going to do when I grew up.

I don't get called by God very often. I struggle to know His will but
direction is so often uncertain. However, there have been crucial times in my
life when I could clearly identify God's pathways. I felt I should not go into
my Dad's business when I had always planned to do so. I felt God wanted me
to stay in Harlem when I wanted to leave. At the end of the sixties I felt God
wanted me to work at trying to figure out how urban institutional systems
could be more responsive to meeting the needs of the poor.

I was sitting in Harlem in the late spring of 1980 thinking about the ghetto
and wondering about my life. After twenty-five years I believed I had some
answers. I was in the midst of some political in-fighting but had found that I
had lost the edge for it. It was then that I felt God directing me to search out
church leaders and challenge them to help the poor. However, after twenty-

five years of concentrating my efforts in the ghetto, I found myself out of touch with ecclesiastical leadership of America. Had I called a meeting, undoubtedly no one would have come. But in faith, I started out on my strange pilgrimage.

I began to call on religious leaders. Each one I saw would provide an entree to several more. Soon I had compiled an extensive list of contacts. I was aided in this task by my qualifications. My experience in the ghetto made me authentic. I also had the advantage of being non-aligned—I had played no part in conferences, coalitions, or movements. I was an Episcopalian who believed deeply in Christ and had been to the ghetto. I was warmly received.

About a month into my journey I began to be aware of a peculiar irony. All my life I had been pleading, pulling, leading, shoving people in the direction of the ghetto. Suddenly, person after person I met was expressing unusual interest in the poor. I knew this was no coincidence.

One night I was in a motel room on a trip to see another religious leader. I opened my Bible and began to leaf through it. Long ago I had underlined in red all the passages that spoke on the theme of the poor. I located the first significant scriptural reference to the poor, a passage in Exodus which recounts God's intentions to deliver His oppressed people.

The Israelis were groaning beneath their burdens. . . . and weeping bitterly before the Lord. . . . Looking down upon them the Lord knew that the time had come for their rescue.
Exod. 2:23-25

For four hundred years the Israelis remained in slavery. Then suddenly the Sovereign God acted. The I AM intervened. The God of history uniquely seized some of it. A burning bush. A confronted pharaoh. Divine miracles. A parted sea. A destroyed army. Jehovah determined to free his people.

Why so long? Why now? Why so much suffering? The natural human inclination is to question. Sovereign acts dominate events. God is here to free his people.

Many centuries have passed. Those extraordinary events have been cast in bedrock for the history of a people and remain a vivid inspiration for the faithful of each generation. Today much of urban America lies in ruins. From a hundred ghettos come cries of bitter defeat. The enthusiasm of the Great Society has been captured by its own failure. Hopelessness stalks the ghetto.

As I read these verses in Exodus I abruptly realized that it was not because of me that people were responding with interest in the poor. God was touching religious leaders in ways that was beyond my human experience. Time and again, people I saw would affirm that God had spoken to them about helping the poor. But they were uncertain as to how to proceed. Then, soon after, they would encounter me. Cornelius had seen a vision but it was Peter who had had to explain it to him. Paul also had experienced a vision.

171

Likewise, he had needed an interpreter. I suddenly understood what was occurring. God, for reasons known only to Him, had chosen this particular moment in history to bring additional help to the American ghetto. I was participating in a breakthrough I had been praying about my whole adult life.

I approached the rest of my visitation program with a new enthusiasm, almost expectancy. I knew that many of the people I would see had already been touched by his Spirit to help the poor. I was merely bringing along some technical assistance. I also had another profound confirmation. I now knew what I was going to do when I grew up.

Whatever God has or hasn't done with my life, He has definitely prepared me to give assistance to anyone who truly wants to help the poor. And that was turning out to be just about everybody I met. I'll never forget one particular week in the late summer of 1980 when a whole series of people responded saying, "Anything you want, we will try to do." The last man was one of the wealthiest men of America. He listened for over an hour. Then he asked if he could pray. He looked out the window of his large skyscraper and prayed for the poor of America. The result of the overwhelming response was a new organization to help the poor. It became known as the STEP Foundation.

In retrospect, one wonders why God did not speak during the sixties in the midst of the urban riots. For several years, the national conscience was moved by these events. But 1969 brought about a mild recession and that brought in turn some fiscal reasons not to do some things that folks didn't much want to do anyway. The rhetoric of the Great Society was retired and the inevitable backlash began to build. The attention of the nation turned away from the ghetto to ecology, Viet Nam, Watergate, gas lines, recession, inflation, the Middle East, hostages, budget cuts, Poland, the Falklands, and so on.

Meanwhile the ghetto continued to erode, capturing new blocks and trapping additional victims in decay. The French have a phrase *les jeux sont faits*—the die is cast. America stands in a world of conflict. The haves and the have-nots battle for survival. Oil and war compete for the attention of policymakers. Inflation and recession challenge the economy. The world seems on the verge of calamity. Judgment seems to have arrived. *Les jeux sont faits.*

But the God of the universe is in control of history. His eternal purpose will be expressed. And in the fullness of time God will act. Perhaps now, as He looks on the American ghettos, He has decided to deliver them and in so doing will speak to his Church and to our nation and the world.

> *"That is the mystery of Grace it never comes too late."*
> Francois Mauriac

Then he said, "This is God's message to Zerubbabel: 'Not by might, nor by power, but by my Spirit, says the Lord of Hosts— you will succeed because of my Spirit, though you are few and weak.' Therefore, no mountain, however high, can stand before Zerubbabel! For it will flatten out before him! And Zerubbabel will finish building this Temple with mighty shouts of thanksgiving for God's mercy, declaring that all was done by grace alone."

Zech. 4:6-7

Section Three
BIBLICAL INSIGHTS

I simply argue that the cross be raised again, at the center of the market place as well as on the steeple of the church. I am recovering the claim that Jesus was not crucified in a cathedral between two candles, but on a cross between two thieves on the town garbage heap, on a crossroad so cosmopolitan that they had to write His title in Hebrew and in Latin and in Greek—at the kind of place where cynics talk smut, thieves curse, and soldiers gamble, because that is where He died, and that is what He died about, and that is what Christians should be about.

Anonymous

The Word became flesh and lived . . . among us . . . full of grace and truth.

John 1:14

This section, called *Biblical Insights,* is a pivotal part of the book. It addresses the critical question: Does the Bible command Christians to help the poor? Your response might be "of course, that is too simple a question." Yet I have spent almost thirty years in the ghetto and have seen little evidence that the Christian community is involved there. Hence my question remains a pertinent one. How do we reconcile the sad plight of the ghetto with the scriptural admonitions to help the poor?

I feel there are two reasons for our failure. First, the Christian community has no plan of action and helping the poor today is complicated business. Second, few Christian folk feel any responsibility for the ghetto. It is almost as if some spiritual guru has given everybody absolution on the matter. The last section of this book sets out a plan of how the Church can help the poor. This section focuses on biblical truths and Christian responsibility.

I would like to take a simple tact in this section. If an athletic team is doing poorly you will often hear the coach say, "We must go back to the basics." The

175

Church is doing poorly in the ghetto. We must go back to the basics.

Is it the responsibility of the Christian community to help the poor? If the answer is yes, then how can the Christian community be motivated to accept its responsibility? On that answer hangs the fate of the ghetto.

I have tried to simply develop some scriptural insights which will help to shape this important answer. Firstly, how extensive is the biblical theme of the poor? Secondly, an attempt to define "Who are the poor?" Thirdly, some reasons why we should help the poor. And finally, some practical suggestions for application.

This section does not represent extensive scholarship on the biblical subject of the poor. I do not have the Hebrew and Greek language training nor the theological expertise. But I don't feel that intellectual discussion is what is now needed. We need to return to the basics and answer some very simple questions. Why teach complicated plays to a team that is not doing simple things properly?

Some critics might suggest that the following material is too elementary. Well, maybe that is the problem. We forgot to start at the beginning. What does the Bible say about helping the poor?

Part One The Biblical Theme of the Poor

The Biblical Theme of the Poor

1 THE EXTENSIVE MENTION OF THE POOR

On the streets they have an expression, "Same old, same old." It's a ghetto description for repetition. There is much in the Bible about the poor.

Life's experiences often make us sensitive to particular messages of the Bible. When someone we love has just died, everything we read in the Scriptures about death acquires new dimensions in meaning. Because of my urban involvement, I became especially cognizant of biblical references to the poor. As I read the Bible, I began to underline passages dealing with the poor. I counted over four hundred passages comprised of over one thousand verses—extensive evidence about a theme that has been neglected by our churches.

The Psalms had the most to say about the poor, followed by Isaiah and Luke. Deuteronomy, Matthew, Jeremiah, Exodus, Amos, Proverbs, Job, Ezekiel, Acts, and Romans also had much to say on the subject. All the books of the Bible made at least passing reference on the theme of the poor except I and II Chronicles, Ezra, Esther, and the Song of Solomon. But perhaps closer scrutiny will reveal what I have overlooked.

If there are so many passages about the poor in the Scriptures, then this subject deserves serious consideration by those who respect the Word of God. Systematic theologians and biblical scholars have generally neglected to develop a definitive biblical "poor-ology" and the people of God lack a reasonable plan of action. This extensive theme of Scripture seems to be as neglected as the poor themselves.

BIBLICAL INSIGHT #1 There are many passages of Scripture that speak to the theme of the poor.

179

2   SOME PEOPLE DISMISS THE ISSUE

While Jesus was in Bethany in the home of a man known as Simon the Leper, a woman came to him with an alabaster jar of very expensive perfume, which she poured on his head as he was reclining at the table.

When the disciples saw this, they were indignant. "Why this waste?" they asked. "This perfume could have been sold at a high price and the money given to the poor."

Aware of this, Jesus said to them, "Why are you bothering this woman? She has done a beautiful thing to me. The poor you will always have with you, but you will not always have me. When she poured this perfume on my body, she did it to prepare me for burial. I tell you the truth, wherever this gospel is preached throughout the world, what she has done will also be told in memory of her."

Matt. 26:6-13

At the outset, I wish to head off a common rationalization for not helping the poor which claims biblical support. In my judgment, the most quoted Bible verse in America today is not John 3:16 but Matthew 26:11: "The poor you will always have with you." It has been employed repeatedly to justify making no effort to help the poor.

Thus when the concerned man says: "We should be helping the folks in the ghetto, they really need our help," he often encounters the objection: "Well, you can't help everyone. You know what Jesus said, 'The poor you will have with you always.'"

But to remove the verse from context is to distort the meaning. Jesus didn't say to his disciples, "Don't help the poor." He said, "Don't do it right now. I'm leaving soon and you'll have plenty of time for that later. Right now give me your undivided attention."

Of course, what Christ said was true. We will always have the poor with us.

But let that be because of the hardened hearts of some self-serving or unconcerned people, or because the poor refuse to help themselves. Let it *not* be because the Christian community has taken no initiative to help the poor.

BIBLICAL INSIGHT #2 **The poor we will have with us always and also the responsibility to help them.**

3   SOME PEOPLE COMPLICATE
THE ISSUE

It is easy to misinterpret the Bible. Most of us don't know either Greek or Hebrew and are untrained in exegesis. We are often unacquainted with the cultures and customs of biblical times. Often careful scholars disagree on the interpretation of the same passage. So what is the average layperson to do?

It was unsettling for me to share the passages about the poor with some seminary professors and students. "You shouldn't take verses from the context of their passages," they warned. "Much of the Old Testament is written to a theocracy and shouldn't be made to apply directly to the present-day Church." "Many of the Matthew passages apply to the future kingdom of Christ." "Often when the Bible refers to the poor it means poor in spirit." "Many of the poor passages of the New Testament refer only to Christian poor."

After some reflection, I offer the following comments: It is obvious that the Bible was written over many thousands of years and we must be sensitive to cultural adaptations. Hardly anyone would bring a sacrificial goat to church on Sunday. We also must be sensitive to God's progressive revelation of Himself in Scripture. The incarnation doesn't come in Genesis, it comes in Matthew. We do need to appreciate and respect the teachings of our seminary professors and clergymen. But God must also have had intended the Bible to be read by the common person. It is the Word of God and all of it is helpful for our spiritual growth (II Timothy 3:16, 17).

The Bible is very important to me. Some of it is hard to understand and interpret, but most of it is plain and simple. When the Bible says don't steal from anybody or Christ died for my sins or study the Word of God or don't tell a lie, I know exactly what it means.

When the Bible says repeatedly that we should help the poor, I can understand that. If some of those verses were written from the perspective of the Old Testament theocracy, and some refer specifically to the Christian poor, we must be sensitive to that. But the teachings and the principles of God concerning the poor are clearly expressed in the Scriptures over and over again. Our problem is not one of interpretation, but application.

BIBLICAL INSIGHT #3 Most of the biblical passages on the poor are very easy to understand.

4 SOME TEACHING FROM THE OLD TESTAMENT

The basic commitment of the nation of Israel to its poor is found throughout the Old Testament. It is firmly entrenched into the law of Moses and the practice of its people. The deviation from those principles becomes the content for the cries of the Psalms and the judgment of the prophets.

> For six years you are to sow your fields and harvest the crops, but during the seventh year let the land lie unplowed and unused. Then the poor among your people may get food from it, and the wild animals may eat what they leave. Do the same with your vineyard and your olive grove.
>
> Exod. 23:10, 11

> At the end of every three years, bring all the tithes of that year's produce and store it in your towns, so that the Levites (who have no allotment or inheritance of their own) and the aliens, the fatherless and the widows who live in your towns may come and eat and be satisfied, and so that the Lord your God may bless you in all the work of your hands.
>
> Deut. 14:28, 29

> Cursed is the man who withholds justice from the alien, the fatherless or the widow. Then all the people shall say, "Amen!"
>
> Deut. 27:19

> Sing to God, sing praise to his name, extol him who rides on the clouds—his name is the Lord—and rejoice before him. A father to the fatherless, a defender of widows, is God in his holy dwelling. God sets the lonely in families, he leads forth the prisoners with singing; but the rebellious live in a sun-scorched land.
>
> Ps. 68:4-6

> . . . wash and make yourselves clean. Take your evil deeds out of my sight! Stop doing wrong, learn to do right! Seek justice,

encourage the oppressed. Defend the cause of the fatherless, plead the case of the widow.

Isa. 1:16, 17

I want you to share your food with the hungry and bring right into your own homes those who are helpless, poor and destitute. . . . If you do these things, God will shed His own glorious light upon you. He will heal you; your godliness will lead you forward, and goodness will be a shield before you, and the glory of the Lord will protect you from behind. Then, when you call, the Lord will answer, "Yes, I am here." He will quickly reply . . . . Feed the hungry! Help those in trouble! Then your light will shine out from the darkness, and the darkness around you shall be as bright as day . . . . Your sons will rebuild the long-deserted ruins of your cities, and you will be known as "The People Who Rebuild Their Walls and Cities.

Isa. 58:7-12

This is what the Lord says: "Let not the wise man boast of his wisdom or the strong man boast of his strength or the rich man boast of his riches, but let him who boasts boast about this: that he understands and knows me, that I am the Lord, who exercises kindness, justice and righteousness on earth, for in these I delight," declares the Lord.

Jer. 9:23, 24

And woe to you, King Jehoiakim, for you are building your great palace with forced labor. By not paying wages you are building injustice into its walls and oppression into its door-frames and ceilings. . . . But a beautiful palace does not make a great king. Why did your father Josiah reign so long? Because he was just and fair in all his dealings. That is why God blessed him. He saw to it that justice and help were given to the poor and the needy and all went well for him. This is how a man lives close to God . . . But you (King Jehoiakim) . . . oppress the poor and reign with ruthlessness.

Jer. 22:13-17

You have driven out the widows from their homes, and stripped their children of every God-given right. Up! Begone! This is no more your land and home, for you have filled it with sin and it will vomit you out.

Mic. 2:9, 10

184

"How can we make up to you for what we've done?" you ask.
"Shall we bow before the Lord with offerings of yearly calves?
No, he has told you what he wants, and this is all it is: To be fair
and just and merciful, and to walk humbly with your God.

Mic. 6:6-8

BIBLICAL INSIGHT #4 The Old Testament teaches concern for the poor.

5   SOME TEACHING FROM JESUS

Against the backdrop of Old Testament teaching that generosity to the poor is sound evidence of the purity of one's faith in God, Jesus stressed sharing one's personal possessions with those in need. Anxiety about food and clothing, He taught, betrays a lack of faith in the provision of God. Consequently, Jesus taught his disciples to look to God for their daily bread. Christ suggested that the truest measure of one's purity of faith in God is often the extent of his willingness to be generous with the poor.

> "You are the salt of the earth. But if the salt loses its saltiness, how can it be made salty again? It is no longer good for anything, except to be thrown out and trampled by men.
>
> "You are the light of the world. A city on a hill cannot be hidden. Neither do people light a lamp and put it under a bowl. Instead they put it on its stand, and it gives light to everyone in the house. In the same way, let your light shine before men, that they may see your good deeds and praise your Father in heaven."
>
> Matt. 5:13-16

> And if anyone gives a cup of cold water to one of these little ones because he is my disciple, I tell you the truth, he will certainly not lose his reward."
>
> Matt. 10:42

> "Teacher, which is the greatest commandment in the Law?"
>
> Jesus replied: "'Love the Lord your God with all your heart and with all your soul and with all your mind,' This is the first and greatest commandment. And the second is like it: 'Love your neighbor as yourself.' All the Law and the Prophets hang on these two commandments."
>
> Matt. 22:36-40

"Then the righteous will answer him, 'Lord, when did we see you hungry and feed you, or thirsty and give you something to drink? When did we see you a stranger and invite you in, or needing clothes and clothe you? When did we see you sick or in prison and go to visit you?'

"The King will reply, 'I tell you the truth, whatever you did for one of the least of these brothers of mine, you did for me.'

Matt. 25:37-40

If someone takes your cloak, do not stop him from taking your tunic. Give to everyone who asks you, and if anyone takes what belongs to you, do not demand it back. Do to others as you would them do to you.

Luke 6:29-31

For if you give, you will get! Your gift will return to you in full and overflowing measure, pressed down, shaken together to make room for more, and running over. Whatever measure you use to give—large or small—will be used to measure what is given back to you.

Luke 6:38

Then Jesus said to him, "You Pharisees wash the outside, but inside you are still dirty—full of greed and wickedness! . . . . Purity is best demonstrated by generosity.

Luke 11:39, 40

Do not be afraid, little flock, for your Father has been pleased to give you the kingdom. Sell your possessions and give to the poor. Provide purses for yourselves that will not wear out, a treasure in heaven that will not be exhausted, where no thief comes near and no moth destroys. For where your treasure is, there your heart will be also.

Luke 12:32-34

When you have a dinner don't invite friends, brothers, relatives, and rich neighbors! For they will return the invitation. Instead, invite the poor, the crippled, the lame, and the blind. Then at the resurrection of the godly, God will reward you for inviting those who can't repay you.

Luke 14:12-14

BIBLICAL INSIGHT #5 Jesus taught concern for the poor

6 SOME TEACHING FROM THE APOSTLES

"I have never been hungry for money or fine clothing—you know that these hands of mine worked to pay my own way and even to supply the needs of those who were with me. And I was a constant example to you in helping the poor; for I re-membered the words of the Lord Jesus, 'It is more blessed to give than to receive.'"

Acts 20:33-35

Up until the time of my careful reading of the Bible I had assumed that most of the scriptural content for helping the poor came from the prophets. I had vivid images of Isaiah or Amos standing defiantly with crooked fingers pointing in accusation while they denounced the social ills of their times.

But to restrict the major social emphasis of the Scriptures to the prophets is to seriously misread the Bible. Its social implications are literally everywhere. Nothing illustrates this principle more graphically than a careful reading of the Epistles. They are filled with directions for a lifestyle of helping those less fortunate.

Though they have been going through much trouble and hard times, they have mixed their wonderful joy with their deep poverty, and the result has been an overflow of giving to others.

II Cor. 8:2

The entire law is summed up in a single command: "Love your neighbor as yourself."

Gal. 5:14

. . . . May you always be doing those good, kind things which show that you are a child of God, for this will bring much praise and glory to the Lord.

Phil. 1:9-11

. . . . So that you will always be doing good, kind things for others while all the time you are learning to know God better and better.

Col. 1:9, 10

In this new life one's nationality or race or education or social position is unimportant; such things mean nothing. Whether a person has Christ is what matters, and he is equally available to all.

Col. 3:11

Dear Brothers, warn those who are lazy; comfort those who are frightened; take tender care of those who are weak; and be patient with everyone. See that no one pays back evil for evil, but always try to do good to each other and to everyone else.

I Thess. 5:14, 15

He died under God's judgment against our sins, so that He could rescue us from constant falling into sin and make us his very own people, with cleansed hearts and real enthusiasm for doing kind things for others.

Titus 2:14-15

Continue to love each other with true brotherly love. Don't forget to be kind to strangers, for some who have done this have entertained angels without realizing it! Don't forget about those in jail. Suffer with them as though you were there yourself. Share the sorrow of those being mistreated, for you know what they are going through.

Heb. 13:1-3

Don't forget to do good and to share what you have with those in need, for such sacrifices are very pleasing to him.

Heb. 13:16

BIBLICAL INSIGHT #6 The apostles taught concern for the poor

7 APPLICATION OF THE SCRIPTURES TO CONTEMPORARY CULTURE

Do your best to present yourself to God as one approved, a workman who does not need to be ashamed and who correctly handles the word of truth.

II Tim. 2:15

The Bible is the Word of God and is essential to our Christian faith and practice. Therefore, the Christian community is indebted to the vast army of persons who have contributed to the handling of the Scriptures down through the centuries. The efforts of these people can be separated into three critical categories.

1. Interpreting—The Bible was written in Hebrew and Greek and by many writers over many hundreds of years. It encompasses diverse cultures and time frames. Scholars have made valuable investigations into the precise meanings of words in particular periods of history. Numerous editions of, commentaries and studies have been written on each chapter of the Bible that attempt to capture the original meaning of the passages.

2. Translating—To convey the true essence of the Bible, we not only must have insights into what words meant when they were written, but also what they mean today. Language changes. The King James Version is not as readily understandable to the layman today as it was in the seventeenth century. The Bible must be constantly retranslated in order to correctly phrase ageless truth in the idiom of the contemporary reader.

3. Applying—The Bible must not only be interpreted for its original meaning and translated into correct language, but it must also be applied. Skilled pastors and wise laymen must challenge their congregations to take the scriptural truths to the needs of their world.

The intellectual leadership of the Church, particularly of the evangelical tradition, has often failed adequately to understand segments of the world to which it speaks. Exhaustive scholarship has been exercised to discover the precise etymological and cultural meaning of the words of Scripture. Enormous publishing efforts have been launched to produce quality translations of the Bible. But the same energy has not been extended in applying the truth of the Scriptures to the needs of the poor.

Very few pastors and professors of the Bible have even basic urban experience. They are "experientially deprived." Most of their time has been spent in suburban churches or seminary classrooms and not in the streets of the ghetto. If every biblical scholar, student and preacher spent one month living among the poor, no church in America would ever be the same. Neither would any poor neighborhood.

It seems strange that God almost never calls trained seminary graduates or experienced pastors to the parishes of the poor where the spiritual needs are so great. The Bible does not lack passages commanding us to help the poor. Rather scholars and preachers have lacked the exposure that would have brought these themes to life for them. Consequently they have overlooked an important part of the Word of God.

BIBLICAL INSIGHT #7 The Bible must not only be understood in its original language and translated properly to modern language but it also must be applied to the needs of the contemporary poor.

Part Two The Poor Defined

The Poor Defined

1 WHO ARE THE POOR?

... He is the God who keeps every promise, and gives justice to
the poor and oppressed, and food to the hungry. He frees the
prisoners, and opens the eyes of the blind; he lifts the burdens
from those bent down beneath their loads. For the Lord loves
good men. He protects the immigrants, and cares for the
orphans and widows.

Ps. 146:6-9

I have made many references to the "poor" in this book. I have
pictured them poetically and I have described my life and work among them.
However, I have not defined the term.

Statistical/Legal Definition of the Poor

Prior to 1935 the majority of the assistance given to the needy originated in
private sector agencies with the Church leading the way. Today government
primarily takes care of the poor. This process was born with the New Deal,
nurtured by both the Fair Deal and the New Frontier and brought to maturity
under the auspices of the Great Society.

As the government has increased its involvement in the inner cities, it has
had to formulate a definition of the poor. Bureaucracies must have rules so
that they can manage the public's limited resources in as fair a manner as
possible. Therefore, many federal agencies employ the Census Bureau's
standard of poverty in their calculation of programmatic eligibility. In 1980,
for example, a non-farm family of four was classified as poor if its income was
less than $8,414 a year. But while it is pragmatic, the poverty index is anything
but a scientific measuring device. There are over one hundred different
calibrations in this code which take such factors as the size of the family,
needs of the geographical region, and other variables into consideration. The
bottom line is that our government can conscionably exclude the working
mother of three who earns $10,000 from its welfare rolls because they
understand that there must be a cutoff point somewhere. Can the Christian
approach the poor in this manner?

194

Perhaps Christians should be immediately discomfited by our welfare system because it represents need as beginning and ending arbitrarily at a statistical point. But, unfortunately, government disbursement of welfare is too often the only dependable poverty program in town. Roughly sixty-nine billion dollars will be spent by our federal government alone this year.* Against this figure, our churches' contribution will seem insignificant.

There is so much about welfare that is distasteful to the Christian. It fosters dependency. It often rewards irresponsibility. It discourages marriage. It creates unhealthy examples for young children. While concerned laypersons have already organized themselves to build nationwide alternatives to public education, they have not demonstrated equal concern in other areas. Few constructive alternatives to welfare have been fashioned by churches. Therefore, the legal statistical definition is by default the only one that is widely operative today.

Popular Conception of the Poor

Most laymen have a definition of the poor that is unrelated to analytical evidence. The bloated-bellied African child and the little Appalachian girl in the raggedy dress demonstrate the type of observable human need with which they would readily identify. Yet this way of characterizing the poor is not without its flaws. Observable human need, while a good indicator of someone's condition, is not always reliable alone as a standard.

Many people claim that American poverty is nonexistent relative to world-wide standards. Our poor have television sets, telephones, apartments and are undergirded by a federal "safety net." Poverty may be more acute in third world countries, but it is still a cruel oppressor in America. Our nation's poor have a different set of problems to overcome because of the ground rules of our society. On one occasion Jesus characterized the needs of the poor as food, shelter and clothing (Matt. 25:35). In an agrarian culture these needs constituted the base necessities of life. But both the agrarian culture and the simple economic relationships of Bible times have passed away. We no longer live in a subsistence society.

Poor Americans, like most of their countrymen, live in an advanced economic system. Ghetto residents cannot slaughter their sheep or harvest their grain when they need food. They must visit a retail supermarket where they are given food in exchange for food stamps or currency. They pay a price that ensures a profit not only for the grocery store owner, but also for those who have handled the food before it reached market. Similarly, a poor urban American in need of shelter cannot pitch a tent in a public park or build a lean-to on a vacant lot. Municipal laws forbid this. The American poor must live in apartments that comply with some form of local housing codes. This requires substantial expenditure.

* The Library of Congress. Congressional Research Service Issue Brief Number IB77069

The elevated standard of living enjoyed by the majority of society has thus imposed certain norms upon the lowest strata. It is safe to say, therefore, that while food, shelter and clothing may have constituted essentials of life in the time of Christ, and in many Third World countries today, in America the list is incomplete. Our less fortunate brothers need an income since they cannot procure food, shelter or the materials for clothing directly from their labor as in an agrarian society. Therefore, they need jobs. It follows that to get a meaningful job in our society, one must have a minimal education. Reading and writing are not optional activities in most employment areas, and are even crucial if one is ever to secure any kind of personal advancement. If Jesus were walking with us today, He might have some things to say about youngsters being sentenced to an adulthood of functional illiteracy. Reading is a skill that is central to a viable subsistence in our culture. Can we comfortably ignore modern needs such as this one?

Biblical Perspective on the Poor

The Bible has much to say on the subject of the poor. Sometimes the term appears as an indication of a spiritual condition. Thus, Christ, who was "rich," became "poor," so that through his "poverty" we might become "rich" (II Cor. 8:9). Still other passages seem to refer to the poor as a social underclass (Luke 14:13). But more often the poor are those who have few possessions and minimal income. For instance, the widow contributed all she had to live "out of her poverty" (Luke 21:4), and one of the passages of Proverbs juxtaposes "poverty" with "riches" (Prov. 30:8).

The Bible acknowledges that the poor will always be present in society (Deut. 15:11, Matt. 26:11). In many cases poverty befalls people because of their own laziness or unrighteousness (Prov. 24:33, 34; Ps. 37:25). However, as I read through the entire text of the Scriptures, I began to notice a consistent mention of the poor as "the alien, the fatherless and the widow" (Deut. 14:29; Ps. 146:6–9; James 1:27). God must have meant something by this grouping. These categories of people shared at least three things in common: they lacked political and legal power in their society, they were involuntarily social dependents, and they were easy prey for potential oppressors. For reasons not wholly under their control, many of them needed special attention.

In the agrarian culture to which the books of the Bible were directly addressed, supporting oneself was normally a matter of selling or trading one's labor. Thus, Paul's injunction to the Thessalonian church: "If a man will not work, he shall not eat." (II Thess. 3:10), implied that healthy men could always work their land or lend themselves out to work that of another. God's special provision did not need to be extended to them. Rather, this was saved for the less fortunate folks. God obligated his people then and now, to be the agents of that provision (Deut. 15:11; Luke 3:11; Gal. 6:9, 10). The Bible, in sum, seems to identify the poor to whom we should pay attention as

individuals unable to see adequately to the satisfaction of their own needs—
for example, widows, orphans and foreigners.

Taking all this into consideration, as a working definition, I will label the
American urban poor as those individuals who lack the ability to improve
their lives and the lives of their children because of a deficiency in food,
clothing, shelter, employment or basic educational skills. The Church has the
responsibility to identify and minister to these needs whether or not the
government or secular society recognizes them as compelling. The example
of Christ and our faith in Him must encourage us to stand apart and seek to
treat the poor as He would treat them.

BIBLICAL INSIGHT #8 The poor are individuals unable to see adequately
                   to the satisfaction of their own needs - for example,
                   widows, orphans and foreigners

Part Three   Some Reasons Why We Should Help the Poor

1. Following the Example of Christ
2. Following the Example of the Saints
3. Christ Meets Us in the Needs of the Poor
4. Opportunities for Spiritual Growth
5. Participating in Human Suffering
6. Being Servants of Jesus Christ
7. Obedience to God
8. Eternal Rewards
9. Escape from God's Judgment
10. A Good Testimony
11. Evidence of Our Love to God
12. The Compassion of Christ
13. To Glorify God

Reasons for Helping the Poor

1   FOLLOWING THE EXAMPLE OF CHRIST

He went to Nazareth, where he had been brought up, and on the Sabbath day he went into the synagogue, as was his custom. And he stood up to read. The scroll of the prophet Isaiah was handed to him. Unrolling it, he found the place where it is written:

> The Spirit of the Lord is on me, because he has anointed me to preach good news to the poor. He has sent me to proclaim freedom for the prisoners and recovery of sight for the blind, to release the oppressd, to proclaim the year of the Lord's favor.

Then he rolled up the scroll, gave it back to the attendant and sat down. The eyes of everyone in the synagogue were fastened on him, and he began by saying to them, "Today this Scripture is fulfilled in your hearing."

Luke 4:16-21

The crowd responded with rapt attention to Jesus' reading. The sixty-first chapter of Isaiah is one of the most moving and powerful passages of Scripture. But then Jesus did a strange thing. He deliberately provoked his audience.

Jesus said that a prophet is not without honor except in his own hometown. There were lots of widows in Elijah's time but the prophet of God was not sent to any of them but to a widow who was a foreigner. There were many lepers in Israel during the time of Elisha yet only one of them was cleansed and he was Naaman the Syrian.

Jesus challenged the crowd at the level of their spiritual commitment. "You applaud my words but don't want to listen to my truth. I have come to preach good news to the poor, to help the disadvantaged, to release the oppressed. The people of Israel in the days of Isaiah were not obeying the law of Moses concerning the poor. But neither are you. God could not work among them. The accepted ones became unacceptable. But He can't work among you either." The crowd was furious at Jesus. They tried to kill Him.

In the tradition of Isaiah, Jesus spoke to the issue of the disadvantaged. He concluded his reading with these startling words. "Today this Scripture is fulfilled in your hearing." The incarnation is here. God has come to visit his world. And what is God like? He is like "preaching good news to the poor, healing the brokenhearted, announcing that captives shall be released, and the downtrodden shall be freed from their oppressors."

But this is not the Jesus we want. Instead, we ask only for pretty words, nice buildings, proper teaching, sound doctrine, great choirs and large Sunday schools. We are all proper and correct. But the real Jesus comes with disturbing talk that threatens to turn our whole lives around, completely rearrange our churches and realign our priorities. We don't want this Jesus of the poor and brokenhearted. We want the Jesus of nice words. We want to applaud. We don't want to weep.

We need to go help the poor because Jesus did. We need to go to the disadvantaged because Jesus told us to. We need to comfort the broken-hearted because that is the way of Christ.

BIBLICAL INSIGHT #9 **The example of Christ is to help the poor.**

2 FOLLOWING THE EXAMPLE OF THE SAINTS

> Whoever heard me spoke well of me, and those who saw me commended me, because I rescued the poor who cried for help, and the fatherless who had none to assist him. The man who was dying blessed me; I made the widow's heart sing. I put on righteousness as my clothing; justice was my robe and my turban. I was eyes to the blind and feet to the lame. I was a father to the needy; I took up the case of the stranger. I broke the fangs of the wicked and snatched the victims from their teeth.
>
> Job 29:11-17

Job was called by the Scriptures a righteous man, the object of special attention by both the devil and God. This passage gives a revealing glimpse of his lifestyle. We often refer to the patience of Job. We should remember to speak more of his charity.

> At Caesarea there was a man named Cornelius, a centurion in what was known as the Italian Regiment. He and all his family were devout and God-fearing; *he gave generously to those in need* and prayed to God regularly. One day at about three in the afternoon he had a vision. He distinctly saw an angel of God, who came to him and said, "Cornelius!" Cornelius stared at him in fear. "What is it, Lord?" he asked. The angel answered, "Your prayers and gifts to the poor have come up as a remembrance before God."
>
> Acts 10:1-4

Cornelius was a Roman centurion whose generosity to those in need came to the attention of God. His lifestyle is a specific and exciting example of charity.

Job was called a righteous man whose acts of charity came to divine attention. Cornelius was a generous man whose gifts to the poor came up as a remembrance before God. Job came at the beginning of God's revelation, Cornelius came much later. Both represent powerful examples of appropriate responses to the needs of the poor.

I would like to emphasize that both Job and Cornelius did more than help the poor. They also properly related to their God. Despite intense suffering, Job never renounced his Creator. It was Cornelius's prayers and gifts to the poor that came to the attention of God and not simply his charity alone.

Job and Cornelius were not alone in demonstrating concern for the poor. We find the same principle imbedded in the laws of Moses, the Psalms of David, the wisdom of Proverbs, the cries of the prophets, the life of Jesus Christ and the teachings of the early church. The apostle Paul said, *"The great leaders of the church who were there had nothing to add to what I was preaching. . . . The only thing they did suggest was that we must always remember the poor, and I, too, was eager for that."*

Gal. 2:6-10

BIBLICAL INSIGHT #10 Job and Cornelius and many other Biblical personalities reveal a scriptural principle of concern for the poor.

3 CHRIST MEETS US IN THE NEEDS OF THE POOR

Now came an argument among them as to which of them would be greatest [in the coming kingdom]! But Jesus knew their thoughts, so he stood a little child beside him and said to them, "Anyone who takes care of a little child like this is caring for me. And whoever cares for me is caring for God who sent me. Your care for others is the measure of your greatness."

Luke 9:46-48

Except for athletic contests and the news, I seldom watch television. But I clearly remember many years ago listening to Bishop Sheen speaking and I will never forget what he said.

As a young priest he helped a girl who had come to New York and run out of money. He had tenderly listened to her tale of woe and he had purchased a ticket for her trip back to Boston. He had returned home internally satisfied that he had been Christ to a distraught human being that day.

He was very tired, but before falling off to sleep he read from the Scriptures. The verse he read said, "And anyone who takes care of a little child like this is taking care of me!"

The Bishop was struck with the passage presenting him with profound truth. "What a blind fool I was. Here I sit with the smug self-righteousness that I was being Christ to a poor distressed young life. And here she was being Christ to me. God forgive me for my presumption."

One of the places that the presence of Christ is found is in the needs of the poor. May God help us to find Him there.

BIBLICAL INSIGHT #11 Christ meets us in the needs of the poor.

4   OPPORTUNITIES FOR SPIRITUAL GROWTH

We can rejoice, too, when we run into problems and trials for we know that they are good for us—they help us learn to be patient. And patience develops strength of character in us and helps us trust God more each time we use it until finally our hope and faith are strong and steady.

Rom. 5:3, 4

I thank God that I suffered through the difficult
it made me reach beyond myself
overwhelmed
defeated
hurt
I cried out for help
as the only meaningful alternative
to survival
without that kind of pressure
I would not have sought
that kind of help
I would have remained self-sufficient

Oh God I know now
why in your wisdom
you sent us to seek the poor
because in that effort
the poor are helped
and we grow spiritually
as we cry out for strength
to accomplish some more of the impossible

BIBLICAL INSIGHT #12 Helping the poor creates difficult agendas from
which come spiritual growth.

5 PARTICIPATING IN HUMAN SUFFERING

The world ignores us, but we are known to God; we live close to death, but here we are, still very much alive. We have been injured but kept from death. Our hearts ache, but at the same time we have the joy of the Lord. We are poor, but we give rich spiritual gifts to others. We owe nothing, yet we enjoy everything.

II Cor. 6:9, 10

The church had been bombed out but now the war was over and it was time to start again. The congregation hired a sculptor to express the hope of the faith through the shape of stones. But they also asked the artist if he could capture some of the pain of a horrible war lest they forget.

The sculptor created a beautiful crucifix artfully portraying the death of our Lord. But within the masonry he interwove ugly pieces of shrapnel as vivid reminders of the price of ultimate estrangement. The new crucifix in the German church realistically depicted Christ's identity with the needs of the world. Such was his mission and ours.

Identification with Christ means struggle. The way of Christ is often the way of hardship. To follow Christ is to participate in the hurts of the world. To follow Christ is to actively seek out human suffering.

Praise be to the God and Father of our Lord Jesus Christ, the Father of compassion and the God of all comfort, who comforts us in all our troubles, so that we can comfort those in any trouble with the comfort we ourselves have received from God.

II Cor. 1:3-5

BIBLICAL INSIGHT #13 Christ calls us to participate in the human suffering of the world.

6 BEING SERVANTS OF JESUS CHRIST

Your attitude should be the same as that of Christ Jesus: Who, being in very nature God, did not consider equality with God something to be grasped, but made himself nothing, taking the very nature of a servant, being made in human likeness. And being found in appearance as a man, he humbled himself and became obedient to death—even death on a cross!

Phil. 2:5-8

Christ has called us to be servants. It is often difficult to be an effective servant. The beginnings of becoming a committed servant is a meaningful relationship with your master.

The great prophet Isaiah begins his writings with these provocative words: "Listen, O heavens and earth, to what the Lord is saying: the children I raised and cared for so long and tenderly have turned against me. Even the animals—the donkey and the ox—know their owner and appreciate his care for them, but not my people Israel."

Once someone recognizes and acknowledges who God is, then it is easier for them to become his servant. The Bible is filled with this kind of spiritual consciousness raising.

Moses had an encounter with God through a burning bush.

Moses covered his face with his hands, for he was afraid to look at God.

Exod. 3:6

Joshua was near Jericho when he was met by the captain of the host of the Lord.

Joshua fell to the ground before him and worshipped him and said, "Give me your commands."

Josh. 5:14

Job was addressed from the whirlwind by the Lord who challenged him: "Do you still want to argue with the Almighty?" Job's response was,

> *I am nothing—how could I ever find the answers? I lay my hand upon my mouth in silence. I have said too much already.*
>
> Job 40:5

Mary received a startling announcement from an angel that she was to bear a child. Mary's humble response was:

> *"I am the Lord's servant". . . "May it be to me as you have said...."*
>
> Luke 1:38

Peter was simply overcome by the size of a catch of fish.

> *When Simon Peter realized what had happened, he fell to his knees before Jesus and said, "Oh, Sir, please leave us—I'm too much of a sinner for you to have around."*
>
> Luke 5:8

Paul was nearing Damascus on a mission to persecute Christians when he was suddenly encountered by brilliant light from Heaven.

> *. . . "Paul! Paul! Why are you persecuting me?". . . "I am Jesus, the one you are persecuting! Now get up and go into the city and await my further instructions."*
>
> Acts 9:4, 5

In each of the biblical references, the spiritual saga takes on similar characteristics: An encounter with the living Lord who was challenging them to respond with a living faith.

But the living faith, once developed, directed the bearer's life. Moses led his people from slavery. Joshua led his army into battle. Job refused to curse God in his sufferings. Mary became the mother of our Lord. Peter became a leader in the new Church. Paul brought the Gospel to the Gentiles. They all became servants of the Lord.

Today, if we are to become his followers we also must become his servants and emulate his example and instructions. Christ was a man of the market place. A man who sought out human need. A man acquainted with the bitterest grief.

He called his disciples to the same lifestyle. They were to be servants who were involved in the needs of the world like He was.

One night just before his death He called his disciples together to share again these simple truths with them. He went around the room and began to wash their feet.

When Jesus came to Peter his disciple reacted strongly.

"No," Peter protested, "You shall never wash my feet!"

"But if I don't you can't be my partner," Jesus replied.

Simon Peter exclaimed, "Then wash my hands and head as well—not just my feet.". . .

Then Jesus said, "Since I the Lord and teacher have washed your feet, you ought to wash others' feet. I have given you an example to follow. Do as I have done to you."

Christ took the time the night before his death to reaffirm to his disciples what their role should be. By the symbolic act of washing their feet He was clearly setting the direction for their future activity. What then becomes very clear is the content of our day—what we are to be about, whom we are to serve.

Any church or any Christian who is not actively seeking out an opportunity to be a servant to the poor cannot possibly be obedient to the Scriptures. Many of the activities that compete for Christian folks' time do not have the scriptural priority that becoming servants to the poor does. Yet for every "Servants to the Poor Committee" there are a dozen "New Building Committees" or "Spiritual Life Conference Committees" or "Choir Presentation Number Seventy-Eight Committees." All these efforts are probably necessary and even scriptural but so is helping the poor and many of our church folks just never get involved.

BIBLICAL INSIGHT #14 **Christ has called us to become servants to the needs of the world.**

7   OBEDIENCE TO GOD

This is love for God: to obey His commands. . . .

I John 5:3

The essence of the Christian faith is divine revelation. God has come to tell us what He is about. The Gospel means good news. God has sent his Son to offer life to the world. Life in Jesus Christ, eternal life. The Gospel is the death and resurrection of Christ—God's offer of forgiveness through Jesus Christ our Lord.

In human terms it would be a more logical Gospel if it espoused good works or human effort. But God's revelation says no one is good enough to qualify for God's standards. Salvation comes through Christ's death. This is the only way. Case closed. We cannot make up our own plan. We accept God's way or we can't participate.

The same ground rules exist for helping the poor. What does God want us to do? What are his wishes? God's principles exist throughout his Scriptures. Go help the poor. Job did it. Israel did it. The prophets did it. Jesus did it. The apostles did it. The early Church did it. Go help the poor. Case closed. To obey God is to go help the poor.

In the Old Testament God told Saul to go to battle but not to bring back any of the spoils. He disobeyed the Lord and kept the best of the sheep and oxen and loot. When Samuel, the prophet, confronted him on his disobedience, Saul said he had only done so to sacrifice them to the Lord.

Samuel replied, "Has the Lord as much pleasure in your burnt offering and sacrifices as in your obedience? Obedience is far better than sacrifice. He is much more interested in your listening to Him than in your offering the fat of rams to Him." The spiritual principle is established. **Obedience is better than sacrifice.**

The Word of God is emphatically clear. The poor are to be taken care of. There is no room for discussion, no avenue for compromise.

But our American ghettos are in ruins, yet they are surrounded by extensive affluence. The ghettos are a giant wart on the face of our land disfiguring our greatness.

The third world countries whose political support and resources are so critical to our future continue to look at America and see so many of their expatriated persons confined to our ghettos. Inequalities permeate our system. They are built into the doorframes of our institutions and the ceilings of our economic structures and the walls of our housing and the pews of our congregations.

But somehow failure to help the poor is not considered a felony by the Christian community. It has somehow been downgraded to a misdemeanor. But God says no, no, no. Failure to help the poor is a felony. And the final expression of God's judgment is yet to come. It is reserved for the mystery and sovereignty of the Lord of Hosts. He will render a conclusion from history and an eternal answer from the edges of time. He commands us to help the poor. It becomes a criteria for our judgment and part of a conclusive statement from the Word of God.

> *See my servant, whom I uphold; my chosen one . . . I have put my spirit upon him; he will reveal justice to the nations of the world . . . He will encourage the fainthearted, those tempted to despair. . . . He will see full justice given to all who have been wronged. . . . He won't be satisfied until truth and righteousness prevail throughout the earth. . . .*
>
> Isa. 42:1–4

BIBLICAL INSIGHT #15   To love God is to obey his commands and He has told us over and over again to go and help the poor.

8   ETERNAL REWARDS

He who is kind to the poor lends to the Lord, and he will reward him for what he has done.

Prov. 19:17

"hey mister"

it was crowded
in Grand Central Station

"hey mister
hey mister"

the man really heard him
the first time
but you don't usually respond
to someone saying
"hey mister"
in a crowded public place

finally
in desperation
the persistent pursuer
qualified his
"hey mister"
with a
"you dropped your wallet"

the facial expression changed
surprised acknowledgment
and genuine appreciation
for the thoughtful act
a thankful citizen
went back to get
what he had dropped

Sometimes what seems to be only sacrifice carries hidden benefits. What apears an untimely interruption turns out to be a pleasant surprise. The poor have so much to teach their volunteers. The lives of each will be enriched by the exchange.

The Scriptures suggest that blessings are in store for us in this life if we help the poor. More importantly, the Bible promises eternal reward for earthly effort. We ought to help the poor because they need our assistance, not because we hope to receive a prize. However, we should remember that God will judge us each according to our efforts.

> *God blesses those who are kind to the poor. He helps them out of their troubles. He protects them and keeps them alive; he publicly honors them and destroys the power of their enemies. He nurses them when they are sick, and soothes their pains and worries.*
>
> **Ps. 41:1-3**

BIBLICAL INSIGHT #16 The Scriptures promise rewards for help to the poor.

9 ESCAPE FROM GOD'S JUDGMENT

Woe to you lounging in luxury ... You push away all thought of punishment awaiting you, but by your deeds you bring the Day of Judgment near. You lie on ivory beds surrounded with luxury, eating the meat of the tenderest lambs and the choicest calves ... You drink wine by the bucketful and perfume yourselves with sweet ointments, caring nothing at all that your brothers need your help. Therefore, you will be the first to be taken as slaves; suddenly your revelry will end.

Amos 6:1-8

You cover your walls, but you leave men bare. Naked—they cry out before your house, and you heed them not; a naked man cries out, but you are busy considering what sort of marble you will have to cover your floors. A poor man asks for money, and does not get it, a human being begs for bread, and your horse chomps a golden bit. The people go hungry, the people weep, and you turn your fingering about. Unhappy man, who has the power but not the will to save so many souls from death.

St. Ambrose

What does the Lord have to say about America today? We have become one of the richest and most powerful nations in the history of civilization, yet from the ghettos of a hundred of our cities come the cries of poverty.

The ghettos of our nation lie in disarray. America is probably the first nation in history to appropriate enough resources to help the poor, and then allow those programs to be so ill-conceived and mismanaged that the condition of the poor is nearly worse for the efforts.

We invoke the authority of the Bible about so many issues of living: abortion, homosexuality, divorce, birth control, and so on. We often develop "stands" based on minimal biblical evidence. Many positions on whole social issues are based upon one or two verses of scriptural evidence. Huge

214

controversies have ripped open the Church because of passages on which biblical scholars disagree.

I am not suggesting that contemporary moral issues do not have biblical support. Nor am I condemning doctrinal controversy as being unjustifiable or unnecessary. Simply, I am questioning why, if we take Scripture so seriously on other matters, do we overlook so much of what it has to say about the poor?

Our Christian communities cry out against abortion and the rights of the unborn, and then leave the babies of the ghetto to grow up in the midst of so little.

We cry out for prayers in our public schools, yet in our urban schools, we allow children to fall four or five years behind in reading levels.

We cry out against pornography on our newsstands and we do nothing about dope on our urban streets.

We cry out about homosexuals and do nothing about the landlords who help turn our cities into slums.

We cry out for armies to defend us from our enemies and we cannot defend the youths in our ghettos from their oppressors.

American society has managed to wall off the poor into large ghettos in large American cities. We have produced twentieth-century poverty zones restricted to those who have nothing else. Some of our Christian leaders decry secular humanism. But who addresses materialism?

The American Church needs to look deeply into its inner cities. Our ghettos are as accepted as our skyscrapers or fast food restaurants. It's business as usual for the American Church. We don't look into the ghetto and see our own neglect. We don't act because we have no guilt. The poor and our faith have little relationship. And we go on singing and fasting and celebrating. And the commandments of God remain unanswered.

> *... You have trampled and crushed beneath your feet the lowly of the world and deprived men of their God-given rights and refused them justice. ...*

Lam. 3:34-36

BIBLICAL INSIGHT #17 God's judgment awaits mistreatment of the poor.

10   A GOOD TESTIMONY

*We try to live in such a way that no one will ever be offended or
kept back from finding the Lord by the way we act, so that no
one can find fault with us and blame it on the Lord. In fact, in
everything we do we try to show that we are true ministers of
God.*

II Cor. 6:3, 4

Paul said that if eating meat offered to idols offended one of his brothers,
then he wouldn't eat meat. Not because he felt it was wrong, but because he
wanted to be sensitive to another's convictions.

Historically the Christian community has taken this biblical principle very
seriously. It has been integral in shaping Christian morality and has led some
Christians to avoid certain social activities. They did not want to be a
"stumbling block" or a "bad witness for Christ."

Various segments of our society, particularly the youth culture, care about
helping the poor. Many of these individuals are not Christians. They are
offended that Christians do not take more interest in these matters. They feel
that the Church does not express enough concern about issues of poverty,
peace, and justice.

And a lot of minority people feel the same way. Some experts suggest that
Sunday morning at 11:00 is the most segregated hour in America.

I will never forget sitting in a room with a whole lot of street people in
Harlem. One of the fellows turned to me and asked, "If your Jesus is the Jesus
of all the people who say He's their Jesus, then how come the ghetto is the
ghetto?"

I was a white man in the ghetto, a Christian amidst what Christians, through
neglect, had helped to create and sustain. I was associated with the under-
the-bushel part of the light of the world. What could I say? The performance
of my Church was a stumbling block to my Christian witness in Harlem.

BIBLICAL INSIGHT #18 **It is offensive to many non-believers and Christians that the Church has not done more for the
poor.**

11   EVIDENCE OF OUR LOVE TO GOD

But if someone who is supposed to be a Christian has money enough to live well, and sees a brother in need, and won't help him—how can God's love be within him? Little children, let us stop just saying we love people; let us really love them, and show it by our actions.

I John 3:17, 18

in some ways
the ghetto is a spiritual mirror
a most disturbing reflection
of our love for our God
look closely into urban blight
and we get some insight
into how much we care
about our Creator
we tend to love
what loves us
we tend to love
that which we respect
perhaps we need a bigger picture of God
before we can make a bigger effort
to help the poor
the Psalmist speaks of his God
as an eternal expression of greatness
one who wears out heavens
like we change a shirt
discarding the old
for the new
with the simple dignity
of who He is
a God worthy of our love
worship
obedience
Job cried out to God
for an answer to his suffering
God's reply is out of the whirlwind

"where were you
when I laid the foundation of the earth?
Do you know how its dimensions were determined
and who did the surveying?
What supports its foundations,
and who laid its cornerstone"
God's answer
is no answer
merely an expression
of his creation
his answer is the final answer
the absolute last word
on the meaning of life
I am who I am
says God
man's response
is not to know
but to respond
and to love
and to worship
and to believe
and to obey
the commandments of God
there is a direct relationship
between loving God
and loving the poor
a specific indication
of spiritual performance
and obedience
the ghetto desperately needs
a new reflection

Do not merely listen to the word, and so deceive yourselves. Do
what it says. Anyone who listens to the word but does not do
what it says is like a man who looks at his face in a mirror and,
after looking at himself, goes away and immediately forgets
what he looks like. But the man who looks intently into the
perfect law that gives freedom, and continues to do this, not
getting what he has heard, but doing it—he will be blessed in
what he does.

James 1:22-25

BIBLICAL INSIGHT #19 Giving to the poor is the evidence of our love to
God

12   THE COMPASSION OF CHRIST

When Jesus landed and saw a large crowd, He had compassion
on them and healed their sick.

Matt. 14:14

Compassion is the capacity to empathize with human need. The life of
Christ is an expression of compassion. When Christ saw the crowds, He was
deeply moved. He wept as He looked over the city of Jerusalem. He was
touched by the blind, the sick, the crippled. He cared for the little children. In
the pain of death, He looked to comfort his grieving mother.

The single greatest reason for helping the poor is compassion. When a
person is filled with God's love and he sees human need, he must respond.

I can walk into a ghetto and identify human need. I don't need a guide. I
don't need government statistics. I can see a love-starved child. I can hear a
young boy who cannot read. I can observe a junkie and understand the pain
of his mother. I can see a pregnant girl and sense the difficulty.

When we see human need with God's compassion we lay aside all Bible
studies, all theological discussions, all talk about religion and introduce a
reality factor. Compassion must respond to identified human need—action
overcomes words, response replaces rhetoric, tears brush aside all creeds. It
narrows down to two things: human need and compassion.

Religion that God our Father accepts as pure and faultless is
this: to look after orphans and widows in their distress and to
keep oneself from being polluted by the world.

James 1:27

BIBLICAL INSIGHT #20 Christ's compassion within our lives compels us
to help the needs of the poor.

13   TO GLORIFY GOD

. . . whatever you do, do it all for the glory of God.

I Cor. 10:31

life was created by God
to glorify Him

Christians help the poor
to glorify God

there is not much
about a ghetto
that glorifies God

little kids without fathers
doesn't glorify God
miles of abandoned houses
doesn't glorify God
the drugs and alcohol
that anesthetize most ghettos
doesn't glorify God
people ripping off a welfare system
crowded jails
inefficient courts
indifferent police
people not working
dirty streets
weak churches
doesn't glorify God

a new way is necessary
additional efforts mandated
the biblical commands are redundant
the Christian response deficient

the racism
the materialism
the indifference
the abandonment
that pervades the ghetto
does not glorify God

our God created all his children
our constitution established freedom
our traditions foster equality
our faith espouses love
but our ghettos divide
our urban streets destroy
God didn't tell his disciples
to stand around waiting for heaven
or a millenium
or a kingdom
He told us to share the Gospel
with everyone
and He told us to love our neighbor
and He defined that
as a Samaritan finding a beat up victim
he had never met before

when Christians love their neighbors
as they love themselves
a system is created
that will abolish anything
that does not glorify God
wars
prejudice
oppression
inequalities
ghettos

BIBLICAL INSIGHT #21 The purpose of helping the poor is to glorify God.

Part Four Some Practical Applications

Some Practical Applications
1   A SPECIAL EMPHASIS TOWARDS THE FAMILY OF GOD

Let us not become weary in doing good for at the proper time
we will reap a harvest if we do not give up. Therefore, as we
have opportunity, let us do good to all people, especially to
those who belong to the family of believers.

Gal. 6:9, 10

This is an important verse of Scripture. It places priority on helping the
Christian poor. But it is also important to emphasize that the verse says let us
do good **to all people**. The believer is asked to specially channel his efforts
toward other believers but he is instructed not to exclude anyone from his
charity.

However, it is helpful to remember that the Church at its inception
represented only a handful of believers. It would have been impractical and
impossible for them to reach out extensively to the poor of the Roman
Empire. They needed to place great emphasis on strengthening their own
small numbers—especially since so many Christian churches were so poor
themselves. Similarly the Israelite nation began with a modest resource base
and only a small group of people. They were surrounded by hostile nations
and had to fight for their survival. It would have been impractical for them to
reach out to the poor of other nations.

However, the contemporary American Church does not face the restric-
tions of the early Church or the Israelite theocracy. We have vast wealth and
resources and claim a huge membership. Christians number between one-
fourth and one-half of the U.S. population, depending upon the definition of
Christian that one employs. The Christian community could and should
reach out to all the poor people of our land. We would have more than
enough to concentrate upon the needs in the family of believers and help
everybody else too.

But to those who want to help the underprivileged believers solely let me
ask if there is a city in America where the Christian community has
constructed a list of all the poor who are Christians. I doubt if such a list exists

or has even been talked about. Certainly, no effective plan has been developed. The Church basically stands disobedient to its Scriptures and insensitive to the responsibilities to help its Christian poor.

BIBLICAL INSIGHT #22 While the Bible says we should do good to all people, it also expresses an emphasis to the family of believers.

2 THERE IS AN EFFECTIVE RELATIONSHIP BETWEEN EVANGELISM AND HELPING THE POOR

Are there still some among you who hold that "only believing" is enough? Believing in one God? Well, remember that the demons believe this too—so strongly that they tremble in terror! Fool! When will you ever learn that "believing" is useless without doing what God wants you to? Faith that does not result in good deeds is not real faith.

James 2:19, 20

It is one thing to stand by the shoulder of the highway and shout to a trapped man in a burning car, "You need to get out." It is quite another dynamic to say those same words as you risk your own life to help free him. There is a relationship between our words and our actions.

I think that one of the reasons God wants us to help the poor is because it creates an effective stance from which to speak the message of Christ both to the poor and the non-poor. There is a relationship between helping the human need and speaking to the hearts of people.

Nehemiah was heartbroken about the condition of his people. He asked Artaxerxes for permission and resources to rebuild the walls of Jerusalem. For decades the walls of Jerusalem lay in ruins. Nehemiah rebuilt them in fifty-two days. The amazing building project became something for all to see—some dynamic evidence of a living faith. The result of the rebuilding of the walls of Jerusalem was a spiritual revival under the leadership of Ezra. There was a direct relationship between the walls of the city and the hearts of people.

Christ doesn't want his words just spoken in the pulpits of the churches, but also in the marketplaces of the city. People with their hands dirty have more of a ring of truth in their voices. That is why the whole concept of the church not becoming involved in social action is such a biblical and Christian distortion. "Social action versus evangelism" is an artificial conflict, **for evangelism happens best in the midst of social involvement.** If the Christian community would go to the walls of the city and help rebuild the ruins of our ghettos, we would create a living proof of a vital faith.

226

Jesus told them, "Go back to John and tell him about the miracles you've seen me do—the blind people I've healed, and the lame people now walking without help . . . and the dead raised to life: and tell him about my preaching the Good News to the poor. Then give him this message, 'Blessed are those who don't doubt me.'"

Matt. 11:4-6

The incarnation was the Word of God. The Word became flesh and lived among us. People not only listened to what He said, but watched what He did. His life breathed integrity and expressed power. Things happened. Jesus' life was unique and bore the stamp of truth. His impact was absolutely earth-shaking.

Since the time of Christ there have been many technological advances. Modern medicine has done much to eliminate disease and improve the quality of human life. Its achievements seem nearly miraculous. Similarly, an elaborate machinery has been erected to reduce poverty. Programs to help the poor can draw upon the latest techniques and ideas in education, economic development, housing, agriculture, nutrition, and health.

The American Church has many resources at its disposal to eliminate aspects of poverty. But its potential has scarcely been tapped. If members of the Church of Jesus Christ entered the ghettos and became "doers of the Word," perhaps they would discover people listening to them as well. And perhaps their actions, collectively, could produce miraculous results. Christ didn't approach his crowds with just words. Neither did the early Church. Why should we?

I dare not judge how effectively He has used others, but I know this: he has used me to win the Gentiles to God. I have won them by my message and by the good way I have lived before them, and by the miracles done through me as signs from God—all by the Holy Spirit's power. In this way I have preached the full Gospel of Christ all the way from Jerusalem clear over into Illyricum.

Rom. 15:18, 19

And so history's greatest event becomes so tragically muzzled—a faith rendered silent by its lack of credibility. And the poor remain the poor. And the Gospel remains the neglected "good news" ruptured in its delivery by the performance of the proclaimers.

BIBLICAL INSIGHT #23 There is a correlation between quality evangelism and helping the poor.

3 GO AND LOVE A POOR PERSON

"Teacher, which is the greatest commandment in the Law?"
Jesus replied: "Love the Lord your God with all your heart and
with all your soul and with all your mind. This is the first and
greatest commandment. And the second is like it: 'Love your
neighbor as yourself.' All the Law and the Prophets hang on
these two commandments."

Matt. 22:36-40

It was late afternoon. The small storefront was filled with youth from
Harlem. Some were studying. Some were being tutored. Others were just
there to be there. A youngster with a serious problem was quietly talking to a
leader in the corner.

Felix had worked in Harlem for a fairly long time and he had some unusual
qualifications. He was remarkably intelligent and caring.

On this particular afternoon, amidst the intense activity of that Harlem
storefront, Felix turned to me and said: "The reason this program works is
because it has **PROPINQUITY**."

I stopped and stared at him.

"Excuse me, Felix, but would you mind please telling me what that word
means."

Felix replied in that soft way of his, "Propinquity means nearness of space,
time or relationship. It is what most bureaucratic institutions are so badly in
need of." I listened carefully to what Felix had to say. The word captured
beautifully what a program for the poor should be about.

And that was what the incarnation was all about. God came to establish
propinquity with his people. He became time. He lived among us. He
entered into relationships. He directly sought out those in need.

The Christian community has not gone to dwell in the ghetto. This is one
important reason why the ghetto is the ghetto. It is in many ways abandoned
territory. We need to go among the poor. We need to form relationships with
the poor. We need to establish propinquity.

But each of us can only handle effectively so many tasks and relationships. Jesus said maximum spirituality is loving others as you love yourself. This can only be attained with Christ's power, and it can only be applied to a limited number of people.

Christ did not heal all the human misery of his time. Nor did He make disciples of every one He met. Jesus limited his physical and spiritual ministry. But what He accomplished was done in God's power and in a quality fashion.

There are so many Christians in America. There are a limited amount of poor people. There surely are as many Christian people as there are poor. If all the Christians in America would just begin to try and love one poor person, the face of poverty in America would be drastically altered.

How much time did the average Christian spend helping the poor last week? Last month? Last year? There is no way that Christian performance in this area matches God's expectation.

In a beautiful passage from Isaiah we are told:

> *Beauty for ashes;*
> *Joy instead of mourning;*
> *Praise instead of heaviness. . . .*
>
> Isa. 61:3

The Christian community must share the message of this great exchange with the poor. We must go to the winos, the junkies, the abandoned, the broken, the lost, the weary, the addicted, the hustlers and tell them the good news. Each one of us could care for one poor person. Beauty for ashes. Joy instead of mourning. Praise instead of heaviness. Praise God on the street corners for joy has come to the block.

BIBLICAL INSIGHT #24 Let each Christian go love a poor person.

4   PRAY FOR THE POOR

But I will rejoice in the Lord. He shall rescue me! From the bottom of my heart praise rises to Him.... Who else protects the weak and helpless from the strong, and the poor and needy from those who would rob them?

Ps. 35:9, 10

the poor are seldom the content
of most public prayer
and I suspect
private as well

and who prays for jails
and urban high schools
and welfare departments
and downtown hospitals

and who prays for the police captain
and welfare worker
the garbage collector
the teacher

and who prays for senior citizen Mr. Smith
and little Alex in the second grade
and "Big Red" who's strung out on dope
and his mother Dottie Clark

O Lord, don't let your downtrodden people be constantly insulted. Give cause for these poor and needy ones to praise your name!

Ps. 74:21

BIBLICAL INSIGHT #25 We must pray more for urban America. Christians can pray even if they cannot do anything else.

5 PART OF ANY CONCERN FOR THE POOR MUST BE INSTITUTIONALLY EXPRESSED

But before I come, I must go down to Jerusalem to take a gift to the Jewish Christians there. For you see, the Christians in Macedonia and Achaia have taken up an offering for those in Jerusalem who are going through such hard times.

Rom. 15:25, 26

The response to needs of the Church in Jerusalem by the Christians in Macedonia and Achaia was institutional. They took a corporate contribution. It went from the Church in Macedonia and Achaia to the Church in Jerusalem. Even in simple times there had to be institutional expression.

Today we live in a highly organized institutional society. It is a product of an advanced technological world. In an agrarian culture a father taught his son his trade. With the growth of technology this became impossible. The educational process has been removed from the home and institutionalized. What happens educationally happens in most areas of society. The care of the poor has now been institutionalized.

Men can't fight tanks. Tanks must fight tanks and not brave men with stones. Individuals cannot very effectively confront institutions. I can personally speak forever on that point. Institutions must confront institutions.

We live in an institutional society. Corporations, school systems, legislatures, unions, trade associations, dominate our everyday life. If the Church is effectively to help the poor, she must do part of that institutionally. The Roman Catholic Church of Poland is an example of the Church making a positive institutional challenge to a secular institution. Despite our numbers, the Christian Church does not have a dominant and concerned voice speaking institutionally for the needs of the poor. It must be created.

BIBLICAL INSIGHT #26 Part of any concern for the poor must be expressed institutionally.

231

6   SUPPORT LOCAL URBAN MINISTRIES

> God did not reject his people, whom he foreknew. Don't you
> know what the Scripture says in the passage about Elijah—how
> he appealed to God against Israel: "Lord, they have killed your
> prophets and torn down your altars; I am the only one left and
> they are trying to kill me." And what was God's answer to him?
> "I have reserved for myself seven thousand who have not bowed
> the knee to Baal."
>
> Rom. 11:2-4

Most Christian urban workers walk alone. They desperately need the
support of the Christian community.

Elijah had had it. It was just one thing after another, a perpetual struggle
with the impossible. And now Queen Jezebel was after him again threatening
to kill him by tomorrow night.

Run Elijah run. Keep going. Hurry Elijah. Flee out into the wilderness
where the hot sun will beat down on your tired head. Finally the prophet
crawled under a bush and prayed that he might die. He had had enough—a
deep death wish expressed by a badgered man of God. He was tired, so very
tired, of his daily struggle in the pursuit of righteousness.

"God," cried out the prophet, "I'm the only one left who still believes in
you."

> Come to me, all you who are weary and burdened, and I will
> give you rest. Take my yoke upon you and learn from me, for I
> am gentle and humble in heart, and you will find rest for your
> souls. For my yoke is easy and my burden is light.
>
> Matt. 11:28-30

What if Elijah and his seven thousand companions in cause could have
ever gotten together? What a meeting that would have been! All those
straight-legged people would have so cheered the old prophet's heart,
sustained him through another round of struggle, stirred the man of God on.

232

The tendency in struggling with the ghetto is to feel isolated and alone. Yet scattered throughout the country, there are many dedicated people who work with the poor. They are buried in school systems, probation departments, police forces, mental hospitals, urban missions, churches and youth programs. Each day they try so hard to make an impact as they struggle against indifferent bureaucracy and impossible human need.

The "critical mass" is out there. Why can't we find them and give them the support of the Christian community. If only this vast army of dedication could be assembled, coordinated and encouraged, what a difference they could make.

BIBLICAL INSIGHT #27 **We need to support our local urban ministries.**

7 WE PROMOTE WORLD EVANGELISM IN ASSISTING THE POOR OF AMERICA

> He said to them, "Go into all the world and preach the good news to all creation."
>
> Mark 16:15

This is the great commission. Christ giving instructions to his Church to take his Gospel to the whole world.

Most of the world does not enjoy America's standard of living. In most Third World countries poverty abounds. In fulfilling the assignment of sharing Christ's Good News with all people, most of those to whom we speak will be poor.

It would seem to me that one of the most important things that we could do for world poverty would be to deal effectively with our own. If in the next few years the Christian community could significantly reduce the poverty in our ghettos, it could free up hundreds of billions for the needs of the world. If the Christians of America ever effectively ministered to our poor, the entree it would provide the Christian community around the world would be almost unlimited. So much of our world opportunities are staked into our domestic responsibilities. If we want to express love to black Africa, we must do so to black Americans. If we want to express love to Latin America, we must do so to Latin Americans. If we want to express our love to Asians, we must do so to Asian Americans. If we are going to love the world and most of them are poor, we must start by loving our own poor. The great commission to the world is the great commission to home.

BIBLICAL INSIGHT #28 If we preach the gospel to the world, we will take it to mostly poor people.

8 ONLY GOD'S GRACE CAN BRING HELP TO THE POOR

God is able to make it up to you by giving you everything you need and more, so that there will not only be enough for your own needs, but plenty left over to give joyfully to others.

II Cor. 9:8

grace is God's answer
to man's response
to divine direction

it is by grace we are saved
it is by grace we are sustained
it is by grace we are protected
it is by grace we are directed

grace is God's undeserved favor
faith is man's response
to God's grace

the whole concept of helping the poor
is so difficult
the idea of changing ghetto neighborhoods
so preposterous
the prospect of defeated lives
finding new hope
so unreasonable
that the whole prospect
can only be pursued
invoking a doctrine of God's grace

the biblical command
is not to wipe out poverty
but to try
our task is not accomplishment

but obedience
and that is a great comfort
in struggling on with the impossible

we should not have
any illusions of grandeur
just the best possible plans
dedicated efforts
and a deep-seated faith
that it is in his hands
our assignment is limited to hard work
results rest with the grace of God

the Bible is filled
with God's resources in action
as we struggle to help the poor
we must claim the grace of God
we have a long tradition
to draw upon

BIBLICAL INSIGHT #29 Claiming God's grace is essential for urban results.

Section Four

A SPECIFIC PLAN

There is a tide in the affairs of men, which taken at the flood, leads on to fortune; omitted all the voyage of their life is bound in the shallows and in miseries. On such a full sea are we now afloat; and we must take the current when it serves, or lose our venture.

William Shakespeare

It is God himself who has made us what we are and given us new lives from Christ Jesus; and long ages ago he planned that we should spend these lives in helping others.

Eph. 2:10

THE PLAN IS DIVIDED INTO THREE PARTS:

PART ONE   PREMISES

I would like to draw attention to several assumptions which provide an important foundation for the plan.

PART TWO   GOALS

The plan has five goals. The steps, which follow, are organized around these goals.

PART THREE   STEPS

The plan consists of 19 steps or activities. They are presented sequentially. One step builds upon the next.

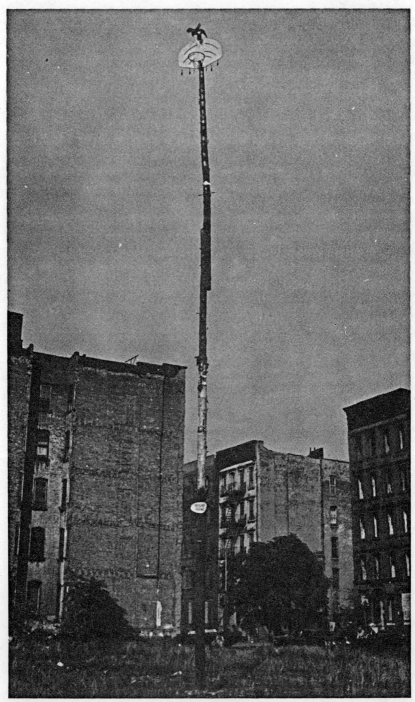

Higher goals

PART ONE PREMISES

PREMISE ONE The Church needs to use new and different strategies to help the contemporary urban poor.

PREMISE TWO This plan, which intends to meet the needs of poor people comprehensively, is a complex one. Congregations must be prepared for this.

PREMISE THREE The people of the urban neighborhood must be involved in all aspects of the program.

PREMISE ONE

HELPING THE POOR IN URBAN CITIES TAKES DIFFERENT STRATEGIES THAN IT DOES IN A SMALL VILLAGE OR RURAL AREA

> When you reap the harvest of your land, do not reap to the very edges of your field or gather the gleanings of your harvest. Do not go over your vineyard a second time or pick up the grapes that have fallen. Leave them for the poor and the alien. I am the Lord your God.
>
> Lev. 19:9, 10

In the Old Testament God provided for the poor by instructing his people to avoid cutting the corners of their field or leaving grapes on their vines—practical suggestions for simple times. But the world has drastically changed. We no longer live in small villages. In an earlier culture, helping the poor was only a matter of commitment. If Farmer Jones' barn burned down or Widow Smith's son needed help, it was simple to know what to do.

However, after the Second World War a boom economy and the automobile helped to create suburbia. In the migration to the suburbs, poor folk were left behind. The result was that the poor, already separated because of possessions and race, became separated geographically as well. A decade later, the Great Society entered the ghetto with energy and expectation, declaring war on poverty. Prompted by the riots of the sixties, huge government appropriations were thrown at problems. Suddenly, in the eighties, the majority of Americans recognize that Federal efforts have been largely deficient. Past failures and present budget constraints have brought our poverty programs to a crossroads.

The task of helping the urban poor is now more complicated than ever. First, the middle class is now separated from the poor. Meaningful relationships and assistance will be extremely hard to maintain. Secondly, the poor are now served by giant institutions with entrenched bureaucracies and largely ineffective programs. The lives of today's urban poor are shaped by these structures: criminal justice systems, educational systems, social welfare systems, medical systems, housing systems, food stamp systems, etc. From the public housing projects they live in to the welfare check they live on,

240

institutions dominate the lives of the poor. No program can really meet the needs of poor persons without dealing with institutions.

Yet the Church of Jesus Christ has not made the necessary changes to update its approach to the poor. If we took a 1980 car into a 1930 gas station, we would encounter some severe technological problems. Much has happened to the auto in fifty years. Jesus once told a parable:

> No one sews a patch of unshrunk cloth on an old garmet. If he does, the new piece will pull away from the old, making the tear worse. And no one pours new wine into old wineskins. If he does, the wine will burst the skins, and both the wine and the wineskins will be ruined. No, he pours new wine into new wineskins.
>
> Mark 2:21, 22

To patch up old clothes or to ferment new wine, we need new materials, not just new commitment. We wouldn't want to run a contemporary bank without computers. We wouldn't fly a modern airliner without radar. Yet our charity remains glued to the past. The results are written across the ravaged face of urban America. The Church must develop new strategies to help its urban poor.

PREMISE ONE The Church needs different strategies to help contemporary urban poverty.

PREMISE TWO

A PLAN WHICH INTENDS TO MEET NEEDS COMPREHENSIVELY IS A COMPLEX ONE. CONGREGATIONS MUST BE PREPARED FOR THIS

> Suppose one of you wants to build a tower. Will he not first sit down and estimate the cost to see if he has enough money to complete it? For if he lays the foundation and is not able to finish it, everyone who sees it will ridicule him saying, "This fellow began to build and was not able to finish."
>
> Luke 14:28

Hundreds of billions of dollars are invested in urban America each year. Yet dividends have been disappointingly meager. This is largely because our efforts have been disjointed. In the ghetto needs interlock and our plans must take this into account. We can no longer afford to pursue piecemeal strategies if we wish to succeed. Instead we must take a comprehensive approach. However, this will add to the complexities of the plan.

Conceptually, a detailed, comprehensive strategy may be difficult to grasp at first. Furthermore, the implementation stage will be complex because simultaneous activity on many fronts requires careful coordination. No broad-based congregation can be expected to have a thorough working knowledge of poor people, mayors' offices, urban workers, funding sources, management structures, drug abuse, private sector agencies, storefront churches, federal funding patterns, attitudes of middle-class minorities and the hundred of other factors that contribute to quality understanding of any potential urban plan. But there is no merit to advancing a simple strategy if it cannot perform its function. Simple plans do not launch spaceships, build skyscrapers, or win military campaigns. Difficult problems usually call for complex solutions.

We must prepare congregations for the complexities of our plan and its implementation. At the outset, we can reassure individuals that they do not have to understand every facet of the program. Instead, a church member should be encouraged to concentrate upon his specific role. The center on a football team does not need to understand all about the quarterback's assignment, nor does he need intimate knowledge of the game plan the coach has developed. But to perform, he must realize what the object and the rules of the game are and must understand his own assignment.

PREMISE TWO The congregations must be prepared for the complexities of the plan.

PREMISE THREE

THE PEOPLE OF THE NEIGHBORHOOD MUST BE INVOLVED IN ALL ASPECTS OF THE PROGRAM

No ghetto is monolithic. No ghetto consists of just winos, drug addicts, welfare cheats, thieves, prostitutes, and other undesirables. There are many reliable and hard-working people on every urban block. There are many people who have a strong faith. Most of these people love their community. That is why they are still there. Not until things get completely impossible—a boiler is left unrepaired, a building is abandoned, or the environment becomes too difficult for their children—do they move on.

Many of these people are older. They remember the neighborhood from a better era. Although, some are afraid to go out on the streets at night, they don't want to move because their roots are there. For many years they have shopped in the same store, worshipped in the same church and known the same friends. Some of these senior citizens are now raising their grand-children. Many still work. Most will die on their block.

Most of the people in the ghetto are not on welfare. Many have the same kinds of jobs that other people have. They are school teachers, nurses, bus drivers, factory workers, sanitation people, probation officers. Others have jobs that no one else wants: dishwashers, domestics, janitors and so on. These jobs are often unattractive but they provide an income. And while single parent families comprise a greater percentage of a ghetto community, there are many solid families and successful marriages. Furthermore, all the students in a ghetto don't drop out. Many go on to college.

People in a ghetto have hobbies, go to cultural affairs, walk their children to school. Many are avid readers. Some participate in politics, own small stores, or serve as officers in their church.

The great tragedy of the diligent people of the ghetto is that they have been passed by and overlooked. They could have become the agents of change of the ghetto. Some have tried. But they cannot do it alone. Massive amounts of drugs infiltrate their neighborhoods destroying so many of their youth. Each day they watch teachers, social workers, police come into their communities and leave. Many are indifferent. Youths drop out of school, landlords abuse buildings, hospitals close down, and nobody does much about it. The good people of the ghetto feel powerless and helpless. They are trapped between indifferent and ineffective institutions and the chaos of the streets.

They are good people. They are heroic people. They fight valiantly, yet they ultimately lose. They are the greatest tragedy of the ghetto. If our society would only organize them and give them the resources, they would save the ghetto. They know who deserves welfare. They would take care of the buildings. They could drive out the dope. But we give them nothing to work with. And so we lose them and their children and the ghetto. The process is happening in the next neighborhood so that some day soon it will also become a ghetto.

But all the while the good people of the ghetto are suffering through their retreat, they never stop reaching out to their neighborhood. They attend the useless meetings, they plead with their children to make it, they provide role models for many of the young to copy. They give advice to the needy and encouragement to the weak. They are the good Samaritans of the ghetto.

If the Christian community is to improve the ghetto, then it must offer itself as the allies of these noble folks. We need their expertise, their vision, their heart. They need our help.

PREMISE THREE **A recognition that the people of the neighborhood must be involved in all aspects of the program.**

PART TWO THE BASIC GOALS OF THE PROGRAM

The Church has retreated geographically and programmatically from the poor. Whole new strategies must be created to bring it back. In my judgment these should be built around five goals:

GOAL ONE   Improve the spiritual effectiveness of the urban church by increasing its resource base, staff, training, facility, etc.
The Church has the ultimate poverty program—the invitation of Jesus Christ to meet our needs. But the urban church is all too often a building in need of repairs manned by a beleagured pastor trying to do it all himself.

GOAL TWO   Concentrate the program first on a specific, small, poor neighborhood.
The essence of management is the development of prototypes. If the Church is going to help the poor, it should begin with a small neighborhood first. Efforts should not be spread over an entire city.

GOAL THREE Review the role of government, private sector and the Church in helping the poor and identify the tasks of each.
With the current budget cutting, certain functions performed by the government may be eliminated. Some of these responsibilities could be performed by the private sector and some by the Church. Specific task definition must be developed.

GOAL FOUR The Church must develop strategies to help the government and private sector in their tasks.
After the roles of each sector are clearly defined, then the Church should help the government and the private sector whenever feasible.

GOAL FIVE The suburban and urban churches working together must

develop programs to implement their specific tasks.
Whatever the Church's tasks become to help the poor, they
should represent a quality effort. Much care and hard work
must be applied in the area of program development.

The laypersons of the Church have the abilities and willingness to develop
and implement a strategy incorporating these goals. But they are sitting in the
pews of our churches like clusters of grapes after the harvest. And harvested
grapes must be used or they soon become useless.

Part Three, which follows, outlines the steps necessary to implement these
five goals.

PART THREE   STEPS (OR ACTIVITIES)

STEP ONE   Find a catalyst in a city who can bring some churches together to help the poor.

STEP TWO   Organize four to seven churches.

STEP THREE   Select chairmen from each church to form a management committee.

STEP FOUR   Call a meeting of a cross-section of the congregations to identify individuals interested in serving the poor.

STEP FIVE   Designate someone from the staff of one of the churches to coordinate the program.

STEP SIX   Find an urban church which can be given the staff and resources to serve effectively its neighborhood.

STEP SEVEN   Develop and survey a specific urban neighborhood around the church.

STEP EIGHT   Expose members of the congregations to the designated area.

STEP NINE   Organize the church task forces.
                    (Description in steps ten through fourteen)

STEP TEN   Form *Friendship Teams* to support those people who work with the poor.

STEP ELEVEN   Establish *Think Tanks* in the congregations to develop work plans for the neighborhoods.

STEP TWELVE   Develop *Skills Task Forces* to apply the skills of the congregation to the needs of the poor.

STEP THIRTEEN   Develop *Ministry Teams* to meet the total needs of poor families.

STEP FOURTEEN	Develop a *Process Committee* for evaluation and public relations purposes.
STEP FIFTEEN	Train volunteers to manage the program.
STEP SIXTEEN	Develop specific spiritual ministries in the neighborhood.
STEP SEVENTEEN	Develop specific programs to meet the physical needs of the neighborhood.
STEP EIGHTEEN	Replicate results of initial prototype into other poor neighborhoods.
STEP NINETEEN	Organize a city committee for restructuring the human service delivery system.

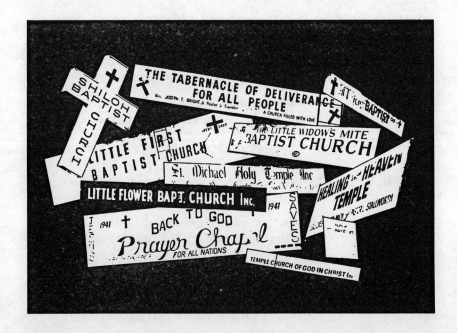

STEP ONE
FIND A CATALYST IN A CITY WHO CAN BRING SOME CHURCHES TOGETHER TO HELP THE POOR

I looked for a man among them who would build up the wall and stand before me in the gap on behalf of the land so I would not have to destroy it. . . .

Ezek. 22:30

The Facts of the Present Urban Situation

1. Massive urban ghettos exist trapping millions of Americans.

2. The urban church is weak. It has not been given the resources to adequately minister to the spiritual needs of the poor.

3. Huge urban institutions that were created to meet the physical needs of the poor have been largely ineffective and have produced extensive dependency.

4. The activities of the average citizen to help the poor have largely ceased.

5. Budget cuts remove the hope of any new monetary assistance from the federal government.

In the light of contemporary fiscal constraints, the only real hope for urban America lies in either using present resources more effectively or from the infusing of volunteers. Both these initiatives are very difficult to bring about. The only institutional force in America today that could possibly provide the manpower and influence for such extensive restructuring is the Church.

The Assets of the American Church

1. The Church has a strong mandate from its Scriptures to help the poor. Obedience to God demands compliance.

2. The Church has at its disposal enormous manpower. It has millions of members.

251

3. The Church has a presence in any urban area. The Black Church, in particular, is a prominent community force.

4. The Church's structure is perfect for organizing and motivating volunteers. Members meet weekly and are naturally divided into many smaller groups such as Sunday school classes, youth groups, women's circles, etc.

5. The Church has a spiritual message and so many of the internal and external causes of poverty are spiritual in nature.

6. Church laypersons are in positions of power throughout the corporate and political structures of the nation. There is little they could not change given the proper plan.

While the Church is a great potential force to galvanize people it must awaken to its opportunity. Each city needs a catalyst—an individual or group of individuals who have the capacity to bring some churches together. The catalyst could be an urban pastor who reaches out to suburban congregations in a non-threatening way. It could be a college or seminary student who spends a summer working in the ghetto and returns home to share his new vision. It could be a businessman, newly appointed to the public housing authority, who begins to see problems in the ghetto for the first time. Every city needs a person or group who can spark activity within the churches.

STEP ONE Find a catalyst to bring together some churches to help the poor.

STEP TWO

ORGANIZE FOUR TO SEVEN CHURCHES IN A CITY TO HELP THE POOR

The Lord replies, "I will arise and defend the oppressed, the poor the needy. I will rescue them as they have longed for me to do."

Ps. 12:5

These churches can come together in a whole variety of ways. An urban church can recruit a suburban one. Suburban churches can find urban ones. One church can call ten churches together and five might decide to work together.

The following are some helpful suggestions:

Composition of the Churches

1. Don't try to organize more than four to seven churches. If you try to organize a lot of churches, you are often limited to your lowest common objection. Let a small handful of churches demonstrate success and you will find many others following the initial attempt.

2. Try to include a variety of denominations among the churches. A broadly based project will attract community support and will have greater acceptance with government and private sector agencies.

3. It is good to have a diversity of size as well. Large churches usually possess more resources. But small churches are easier to organize.

4. There should be basic theological affinity between the churches. This leads to greater unity and spiritual strength.

5. One of the churches should be a minority middle-class congregation. They will provide important insights into all activities.

6. One of the churches must be located in the poor section of town where the initial project will be located. This church will become the spiritual base for the program and the site from which many of the resources will be distributed.

An Important Reminder

It is essential that each cooperating church retain its own identity. Members and staff will respond most enthusiastically when working under their own church and not under a consortium. However, certain tasks can be best accomplished by a group of churches. For example, influence can be maximized when it is exercised by broad-based coalitions. Also, idea development may benefit if churches think collectively. Such collective efforts only increase the effectiveness of an individual church effort.

STEP TWO Organize four to seven churches.

STEP THREE

SELECT CHAIRMEN FROM EACH CHURCH AND HAVE THEM MEET TO FORM A MANAGEMENT COMMITTEE WHICH GIVES LEADERSHIP TO THE PROJECT

Each pastor should select a chairman who will give leadership in his church. The chairman should be respected within the church, have good management skills, and be able to inspire the church to get involved in the project. Enthusiasm and ability to plan long-range are also essential qualities for the chairman because the problems of the inner city will not be solved overnight.

The chairman must be able to challenge the church, relying on the pastor's spiritual guidance and ministry. He will need the pastor's support in ensuring that his church understand what the Scriptures have to say about the relationship of the church to the poor.

The chairmen from each church should meet every two weeks as an executive committee for the project. This meeting is an important time of problem-solving, coordination, spiritual fellowship, and decision-making. Representation from the local inner-city church at this meeting is imperative as decisions are made on how resources will be delivered to the inner-city neighborhood. This executive committee should provide strong leadership for the project as a whole and encourage pastors and other interested people to attend its meetings.

STEP THREE Select chairman from each church to form a management committee.

STEP FOUR

CALL A MEETING TO ORGANIZE THE PROGRAM TO HELP THE POOR

Philip found Nathanael and told him, "We have found the one Moses wrote about in the law, and about whom the prophets also wrote—Jesus of Nazareth, the son of Joseph."

"Nazareth! Can anything good come from there?" Nathanael asked.

"Come and see," said Philip.

John 1:45, 46

Philip told Nathanael he had found the Messiah. Nathanael's first reaction was doubt. Philip wisely advised him, "Come and see."

In order to begin a successful volunteer program, invite a group of about one hundred parishioners to a meeting. It would be best if they represent a cross-section of the congregation. Within any congregation are many people just waiting to come and help the poor. The task is to find out who they are. By exposing them to the problems and the plan, they will identify themselves. *Don't* be tempted to talk anyone into participating. Let people volunteer. Don't play upon their sense of guilt. Guilty people make inconsistent servants.

A qualified person should make a presentation to the group. This should include a description of the needs of the poor, specific mention of the scriptural commands to help the poor and a basic outline of the plan. Many people have wanted to help the poor for years and have only awaited the opportunity. Give them one.

STEP FOUR Call a meeting.

STEP FIVE

DESIGNATE SOMEONE FROM THE STAFF OF ONE OF THE CHURCHES TO COORDINATE THE PROGRAM

But with the believers multiplying rapidly, there were rumblings of discontent. Those who spoke only Greek complained that their widows were being discriminated against, that they were not being given as much food, in the daily distribution, as the widows who spoke Hebrew. So the Twelve called a meeting of all the believers. "We should spend our time preaching, not administering a feeding program." "Now look around you among yourselves and select seven men, wise and full of the Holy Spirit, who are well thought of by everyone; and we will put them in charge of this business. Then we can spend our time in prayer, preaching, and teaching."

Acts 6:1-6

The first church deacons were appointed because of controversy. The Greek contingent felt their widows weren't getting the same amount of food as the Jewish speaking ones. They complained to the apostles. The result was an administrative decision to create the new position of deacon and divide labor. The apostles were to spend their time in prayer, preaching and teaching. Deacons were to minister to the needs of the body of believers.

Helping today's poor is complicated business. Because of the geographical separation and institutional character of contemporary poverty, the Church must create new positions to meet new needs. The Church has failed to channel the skills of laymen toward the needs of the poor. This is largely because religious leaders rarely have a good working knowledge of either the skills of their laymen or the needs of the poor.

Occupational skills have become so diverse and specialized that ministers have difficulty understanding, let alone assessing, the professional expertise of their congregations. One individual is called upon to minister effectively to the advertising man, the surgeon, factory-worker, housewife, and retired

257

executive. The burden upon the minister is compounded if he is also asked to broker his congregation's skills to the poor.

Similarly, the average religious leader has an increasingly difficult time keeping pace with the myriad of institutions which have been created to meet the needs of the poor. Welfare programs, jails, urban education, and drug programs are often as confusing to religious leaders as they are to their congregations.

The average religious leader is not to be faulted for incomplete knowledge of either his congregation's skills or the ghetto's need. The demands upon him are so great that he would not have time to act upon that knowledge if it were complete.

But cruel waste results from this non-involvement. The needs of the poor go unmet and the skills of laymen go unexpressed. Laymen begin to say, "My religious experience is irrelevant," and the poor say, "The Church doesn't care."

If the Church is to minister successfully to the ghetto, new responsibilities must be created. We need people to act as mediators between the needs of the poor and the skills of the congregation. It is not only needed, it is scriptural. The tasks of the deacons must be upgraded. Millions of laypersons are waiting to help.

In order to facilitate this process, we need a leader. It is likely that one of the suburban churches in your program is large enough to have a staff of ministers. One of these ministers will probably have responsibility for community programs or adult ministries. If so, this minister is in an ideal position to assume responsibility for the administration of the program. It would only enhance his present responsibilities. In this way, management is given to the program without increasing its cost.

STEP FIVE **Designate someone from the staff of one of the churches to coordinate the entire program.**

STEP SIX

FIND AN URBAN CHURCH WHICH CAN BE DEVELOPED INTO A NEIGHBORHOOD FORCE

If we want to assist poor people, we must strengthen their congregations. Destruction of the work ethic, drug and alcohol abuse, crime, abandonment of family and many other aspects of poverty are rooted in spiritual deficiency. Any meaningful urban strategy must be grounded upon strengthening the urban church.

STATE OF THE CONTEMPORARY URBAN CHURCH

Urban Churches Can Be Divided Into Five Categories

1. **The Old Historic Downtown Church**
    Many large churches near the downtown area of cities have strongly functioning congregations. They were originally constructed in the middle of wealthy residential sections from which people have long since moved. These churches have survived because of what they had at the peak of their influence. They have impressive buildings, endowments of some form, and often older but very loyal parishioners. Many have also had a long list of impressive preachers who have attracted worshipers from all over the city. With the rebirth of urban downtown centers and condominium complexes, a new affluent urban dweller is beginning to fill their pews. Many of these churches are now on very valuable land and are often surrounded by corporate sky-scrapers. These churches have enormous potential to help poor people. Many of them are doing so, but they are not the churches of the poor.

2. **The Urban Church Held Together by an Edifice**
    Many urban churches with impressive buildings and past histories did not manage to survive the years very well. They are still held together by an aging congregation but the years have been painful. Now the church sits with a congregation of elderly parishioners who want to be left

259

alone until they die. Their future rested in reaching out to their new neighbors. This they never did. They also refused all offers to purchase the building, which now exists as a fortress protecting their dying mentality.

3. **The Middle-Class Minority Urban Church**
   Some minority middle-class churches were formed when white folks moved out, took their congregations with them and sold the building to minority folk. Some minority middle-class churches are old historic ones that can trace their beginnings back to old colored sections of town. Upward mobility has allowed many of their members to move to better neighborhoods, but unlike the white folks, they are not afraid to drive back into their old neighborhoods. Very few people from the neighborhood ever come to this church. So while these churches represent solid middle-class minority congregations, they are having little impact on the poor that surround their building.

4. **The Struggling Urban Church**
   This is also a church of basically middle-class minority people who no longer live in the neighborhood but drive in each Sunday. But unlike some of its sister minority congregations, it never prospered. There are thousands of these kinds of inner-city churches scattered throughout the poor neighborhoods of urban America. Most are mired down with few resources as a hundred or so members try to keep the church going. They realize little growth and demonstrate almost no active ministry to the blocks that surround their building.

5. **The Storefront Urban Church**
   These are small congregations of poor people worshipping in a storefront or house. Some grow into larger forms; most remain a vehicle of religious expression for a handful of poor people many of whom are women.

Some Observations:

1. Except for the storefront church, most of the members who come to worship on Sunday morning in urban churches do not live in the area. They drive to church on Sunday and return home when the service is over.

2. The urban church conveys almost no impact on the institutional structures of its neighborhood (schools, police, etc.).

3. They conduct few aggressive attempts to meet the spiritual needs of the neighborhood.

4. During the week, the urban church initiates little activity of any kind in

its neighborhood. Many urban churches are, in effect, locked up from Sunday to Sunday.

5. Many of the smaller churches have pastors who work full or part-time elsewhere and only have limited time to develop their churches.

6. Middle-class minority families have their own legitimate spiritual needs to meet. Their churches are probably not the best structures from which to reach out to extensive numbers of street people. Because of the middle-class orientation of these congregations, someone who is dirt poor, or on welfare, or messed up on drugs is probably not going to feel comfortable within them. The music, the style of worship, the dress of the parishioners, the language of the minister are more geared to the upwardly mobile congregation. These churches, however, represent a spiritual and resource base and provide role models which are essential to the development of a vital ministry to the urban poor. But they usually will not be the means or vehicles to reach and to take care of the poor themselves. The most expedient way to reach the poor people is to create something just for them, not to try to fit them into a middle-class institution.

7. There are many exciting exceptions to the above observations.

PROPOSED SOLUTION

The struggling urban church or some storefront churches represent, in my opinion, the greatest potential to bring immediate assistance to the poor people in the ghetto. Every major American city will have dozens of churches which fit into this category. Many are pastored by good people who, if they only had a little bit of help, could attract hundreds and hundreds of poor people to their congregations. This is where the Christian community must focus its efforts and bring to fruition a new kind of vital urban church—one whose whole effort is directed toward reaching the poor.

STEP SIX Find an urban church which can be given the staff and resources to serve its neighborhood effectively.

STEP SEVEN

DESIGNATE AND SURVEY A SMALL NEIGHBORHOOD AROUND THE URBAN CHURCH. CONCENTRATE ALL EFFORTS INTO A FEW BLOCKS

Good management demands the development of prototypes. General Motors can make a million cars because they can make one. Singer can make a million sewing machines because they can make one. We would never build a new tank without a working model. If this management technique has been successful for the Department of Defense, why can't it be used in our social efforts? Yet we pour billions of dollars into novel urban systems without demanding prototypes. The results are written across the scarred face of urban America.

If prototypes are recommended at Harvard and perfected at IBM the Christian community can create them in Harlem. Let us take ten or twenty blocks of a poor neighborhood in cities across America and make them work. Let us take a couple of neighborhoods and pour life back into their streets. Let us consecrate those streets to God and mobilize the best brains in Christendom to figure out how to improve them.

What makes a great grade school? What makes a great hospital? What makes a great police precinct? A great post office? A great welfare structure? A great high school? Park? Sanitation system? Probation office? Housing project? Junior high school? Neighborhood business? Christians from all over a city, come give your answers. Your insights. Your experience. Teachers, police officers, welfare workers, social workers, probation officers, nurses, people who live in the neighborhood, come give your ideas to these blocks. Give them to God. Managers, administrators, come tell us how it should all fit together. Produce a holy grid. Then we will take our successful model and transplant it to every poor section of each city in America.

This process begins by designating a specific urban neighborhood and performing a comprehensive survey of the area to identify all schools, churches, and existing community programs within its perimeter. A detailed map should be drawn up, all housing would need to be inventoried, all small businesses assessed, census data procured and so forth. Work in the selected area should not begin before a thorough analysis of existing resources and activities is made.

STEP SEVEN   Designate and survey a specific urban neighborhood around the urban church.

STEP EIGHT

EXPOSE MEMBERS OF THE CONGREGA-TIONS TO THE DESIGNATED AREAS

The most effective way to change attitudes about the poor is to expose people to human need. People tend to respond best to what they can see. My own commitment to the poor is largely based upon my experience in the ghetto. I knew for years what the Bible had to say about helping the poor. But it was only when I lived among the poor that I began to respond to their condition.

I have given thousands of tours of the ghetto. They never fail to convince folks of needs and bring out new commitments. After congregations are exposed to the plan, take them to see the designated area and let them talk with the people from the blocks and the urban neighborhood.

However, don't limit tours to the beginning of the program. Continue to run them. Suggest that all prospective members come see the ghetto as a requirement of joining the church. As the program progresses, volunteers will find themselves going into the ghetto frequently. Perhaps they will want to invite friends to accompany them. This kind of trip can function both as tour and mission of mercy. Gradually, the ghetto neighborhood will become more a place to be involved in and less a place to observe. Tours will take on a more positive character; their principle object will be to demonstrate progress.

STEP EIGHT Expose members of the congregations to the designated areas.

STEP NINE

ORGANIZE THE CHURCH TASK FORCES

> Just as each of us has one body with many members, . . . so in
> Christ we who are many form one body. We have different gifts,
> according to the grace given us. . . . If it is serving, let him serve;
> if it is teaching, let him teach; if it is encouraging, let him
> encourage; if it is contributing to the needs of others, let him
> give generously; if it is leadership, let him govern diligently; if it
> is showing mercy, let him do it cheerfully.
>
> Rom. 12:4-8

If we want to help the urban poor successfully, we must do it with careful organization. For several years I have had an opportunity to experiment with congregations in structuring such help. I do not share my observations as a conclusion, but rather to suggest a point of departure.

Simplicity of Design

It is essential to keep things simple. The average church member doesn't have time to attend additional meetings or become a part of a new committee. Efforts should be made through the existing organizations of the church—women's groups, Sunday school classes, youth groups. Helping the poor should be on the agenda of most church organizations anyway.

Although excessive committees are to be avoided, careful structure is needed. Organization of the congregation can be accomplished by establishing task forces with clear objectives. An active chairman can supervise their functions. Task forces don't need to meet often. Most of their duties can be performed informally—phone conversations, written directives, brief meetings before or after other meetings.

A Chairman

The need for a chairman has been mentioned in step three. The chairman's task in each church is to coordinate five task forces. The suggested task forces are as follows:

Friendship Task Forces

These task forces have the responsibility first, for relating to the institutional leaders of the community and second, to all public servants who want their assistance. Essentially, they are influence committees composed of people of the congregation who have been successful in their professional endeavors and are willing to share themselves and their abilities.

This task force should:

(1) Establish relationships with institutional leaders in the community such as the high school principal, the police precinct captain, the head of a welfare office, and the urban pastor. The task force should meet with them on a monthly basis to lend support and to listen to their needs and problems. Other friendship members would meet with individual public servants—teachers, welfare workers, etc.

(2) Communicate these needs and problems to the research task force (Think Tanks).

(3) Act as a constant communication link throughout the problem solving and resource procurement process.

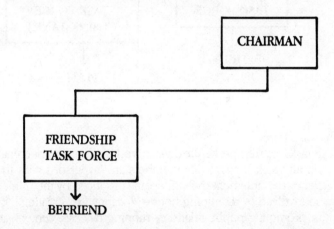

Research Task Force (Church Think Tank)

This task force represents the creative cutting edge of the congregation in such areas as education, health, management, law enforcement, recreation, etc. It attempts to solve the problems and needs expressed by the institutional leaders through the activities of the friendship committees.

The Research task force should:

(1) Develop work plans in various content areas of the think tank such as education, jobs, etc., that can be implemented by the skills task forces of the congregations.

(2) Respond to the requests of the institutional leaders conveyed through the friendship task force.

(3) Tap the creative resources of the congregation to explore new solutions to urban problems. For example:

- A new data processing procedure could be developed to take school attendance.

- A new supplemental curriculum for second grade math could be devised.

- The food menu of an urban high school cafeteria could be upgraded.

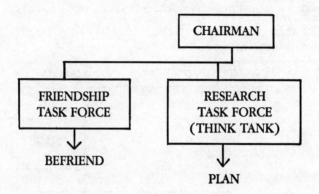

Skills Task Force

This task force represents the diverse work skills of the congregation (what they do all week long). Skills members are laypersons with the practical proficiency to implement the work plans produced by the think tank. They may be involved in rebuilding houses, locating and creating jobs, tutoring youths, promoting public relations, running day care centers, accounting, and performing preventive medical assistance.

The Skills task force should:

(1) Inventory the work skills of the congregation.

(2) Implement the work plans of the research task force or church think tanks. For example:

- An accountant could help to upgrade the financial records of several small community businesses.

- An electrician could help with some new wiring.

- A lawyer could defend a youth in court.

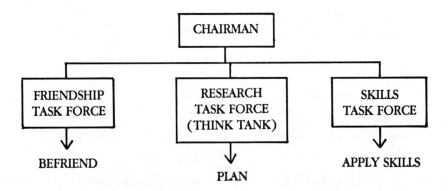

Ministry Task Force

These individuals are responsible for ministering to the spiritual needs of the poor, working wherever possible through families.

The Ministry task force should:

(1) Develop ministry teams to befriend families and to assist them in implementing prescriptions of personal inventory teams. Ministry teams wold consist of two couples for each targeted family.

(2) Develop personal inventory teams of an educator, jobs person, financial specialist, social worker, and spiritual person to ascertain the comprehensive needs of a family or individual and write prescriptions based upon work plans of think tank.

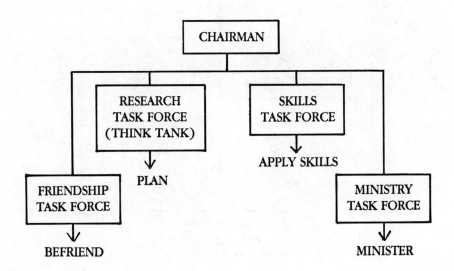

Process Task Force

This task force has two major responsibilities:

(1) Quality control and evaluation of the program.

(2) Advertising and promoting the program.
Some examples:
- Taking members of the congregation on tours of the ghetto.

- Producing newsletters to the congregation, bulletin inserts, etc.

- Performing an evaluation of a tutoring project.

- Making recommendations for improving the quality of the training of volunteers.

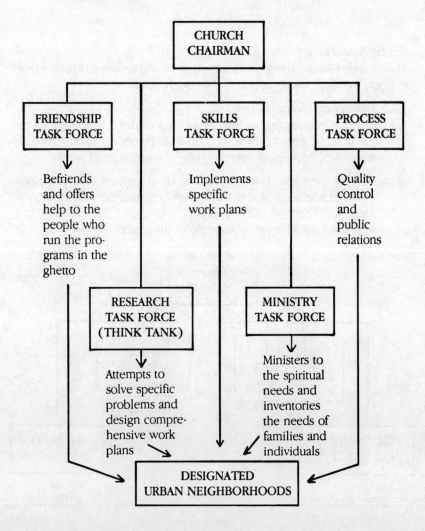

A Joint Effort

No church will have sufficient resources to change an urban neighborhood single-handedly. Nor will any one church have the diversity of gifts to implement such a comprehensive project. Groups of congregations must work together. This is not a legal agreement. It is simply four to seven churches agreeing to cooperate to help the poor in a geographical neighborhood. If someone wants to drop out or be added—so be it.

Additional Support Churches

Once four to seven churches are highly organized with task forces, other churches can join the effort in supportive ways. These additional churches could help by expanding the friendship teams, think tanks, work plans, spiritual ministries and process task forces that have been created.

The purpose of this organizing effort is to give every participant a specific task to do. Unless such a management strategy is followed, specific skills of laypersons will never be applied to the specific needs of the urban poor. When people live miles apart and public institutions dominate human service delivery systems either you intensively organize assistance or you frustrate volunteer effort. Our urban productivity will directly correspond to our organization.

STEP NINE **Organize the church task forces.**

STEP TEN/PART A

DEVELOP FRIENDSHIP TASK FORCES TO HELP THOSE PEOPLE WHO WORK WITH THE POOR

God is able to make it up to you by giving you everything you need and more, so that there will not only be enough for your own needs, but plenty left over to give joyfully to others.
II Cor. 9:8

Some of the people in the best position to shepherd the poor are the people who work in the institutions: the teacher, the policeman, the postman, the welfare workers, the probation workers. All receive little support and encouragement and must work under conditions of great stress. Consequently, they often become discouraged and defeated persons.

This then becomes an additional tragedy of urban instititions—the damage that they have inflicted on the persons who staff those structures. If you feel defeated personally, you cannot be a quality shepherd. Institutional life in urban America consists of so many hurting people. Staff and clients often resemble the wounded waiting for someone to care and notice them. They are neglected and starved for attention. Their expectations have been bruised and it is expressed in their attitudes.

The Christian community needs to bolster these institutional shepherds of the poor with friendships. It can be done in a natural and meaningful way if we will organize effectively. Specific members of congregations need to relate to specific institutional workers. Mr. Smith, from St. Joseph Methodist Church, needs to befriend Officer Harry. Nancy, from the Second Baptist Church, needs to befriend Mrs. Jones, the second grade teacher, and so on.

We must not only befriend the urban workers, but we must also assist them in practical ways depending upon their individual needs and opportunities: flowers for the shut-ins on the postman's tour, some independent study programs for the teacher, a trip to somewhere exciting for some youth on the policeman's beat, some jobs for the welfare worker.

Representatives of the church will go to the principal, the welfare supervisor, and the police sergeant, and say, "What can we do to help? Give us your problems and we will go back to our congregations and see what we can do."

His response may be:

"No one comes to my PTA . . ."

"I would like to explore ways in which data processing can be used in my school . . ."

"There is no responsible job development going on in my welfare offices . . ."

"My police officers need to be better trained in human relations . . ."

"There are no garbage containers in the ghetto so everyone throws their papers on the sidewalk . . ."

The lists will be endless. So will the opportunities to help.

One of the most sensible strategies to help the poor is to support the people who work with them. This approach can effectively involve a number of people who would ordinarily become unnerved at the thought of going into a poor area of town and working directly with the people there. Most church members feel more comfortable and better equipped to help public servants. They have much more in common with public servants than poor folk. Perhaps they even attend the same suburban church.

Surrounding the people who man the agencies and institutions with support and concern is a vital and effective way for the church to help the poor.

Procedure

1. Friendship task force chairman organizes friendship teams of five people from different churches who surround the leaders of institutions who work with the poor. Other teams of one or two laypersons are also organized to befriend individual public servants.

2. Friendship committees should meet on a monthly basis with the urban workers and leaders working with a list of their immediate needs and long-range vision.

3. Friendship committee members should look for natural and meaningful ways to befriend their urban worker. (Visits to his place of work, invitation to a social event, phone calls, etc.)

4. The needs are reported to think tanks for development and the friendship committee monitors all progress.

STEP TEN Form friendship teams to help those people who work with the poor.

Officer Harry needs his Friendship Task Force

STEP TEN/PART B

A NEED LIST FROM A JUNIOR HIGH SCHOOL PRINCIPAL WHICH WAS PRESENTED TO A FRIENDSHIP COMMITTEE

1. The food in the cafeteria needs upgrading.

2. I would like to have a band in my school.

3. It takes so long to receive books and supplies that my teachers order.

4. I would like a computer for students to become acquainted with.

5. One of the teachers has a drinking problem. I don't exactly know how to handle it.

6. My students seldom have field trips.

7. I would like a few small trophies.

8. I would like some prizes for our attendance contest.

9. I would like my students to be exposed to a college campus. They never see one.

10. Math manipulatives for all grades: calculators, measuring tools, etc.

11. Sports equipment.

12. Inexpensive cameras.

13. Library and reference books.

14. Professional art supplies.

15. Consultants in all fields for our career education program.

16. My PTA needs help. Almost no one comes.

17. Help to locate used scientific equipment from industry or universities that could be used in our science labs.

18. People in industry who could help with lectures, field trips and/or tours of facilities.

STEP TEN/PART C

A NEED LIST FROM A DIRECTOR OF PUBLIC HOUSING PROJECT WHICH WAS PRESENTED TO A FRIENDSHIP COMMITTEE

1. More recreation for teenagers.

2. Crime-watch; security or police department patrol.

3. Employment assistance for residents.

4. Have residents involved to help protect housing authority property.

5. Teach residents how to perform preventive maintenance.

6. Have more activities for senior citizens.

7. Provide adult basic education for illiterate people and training for GED, (Graduate Equivalency Diploma)

8. Provide resource persons for handicapped residents.

9. Promote community pride with emphasis on voting, representations on issues of concern to residents, and response to community needs.

10. Assist resident council officers create activities to generate funds.

11. Promote communication between management and residents.

12. Serve as a liaison between parties involved.

13. Communicate with housing authority administration the need to eliminate poor living conditions for residents.

14. Provide assistance in all areas of maintenance.

15. Invite special guests for all residents' activities.

16. Provide transportation for all activities.

17. Plan for other activities besides sports.

18. Be able to help office staff cope with various tasks to eliminate high rate of turnover.

19. Provide staff training and development for purpose of motivation.

20. Improve physical appearance of management offices.

STEP ELEVEN/PART A

ORGANIZE THE THINK TANK TO CONDUCT RESEARCH IN TEN CONTENT AREAS

When the poor and needy seek water and there is none and their tongues are parched from thirst, then I will answer when they cry to me . . . In the deserts will be pools of water, and rivers fed by springs shall flow across the dry, parched ground. I will plant trees . . . on barren land. Everyone will see this miracle and understand that it is God who did it. . . .

Isa. 41:17-20

We need a blueprint if we are to change poor neighborhoods. A plan begins with a need assessment. Since a ghetto is the sum of its parts, any attempt to change the whole must involve a strategy to improve each piece. I have found it useful to sketch the anatomy of the ghetto in terms of ten content areas of need.

1. **Education** Most urban youth are far below the national average in reading levels and scholastic achievement. How do you perform quality education without the undergirding of a family structure?

2. **Recreational/Cultural Activites** Unkept parks, unsafe streets, inadequate cultural opportunities characterize many of our poor neighborhoods.

3. **Criminal Justice Systems** Today's courts are often hopelessly backlogged and staffed by indifferent, even cynical personnel. Many jails have become overcrowded. How do you reduce crime in a culture that has so many youths who have no hope?

4. **Drugs** Why should drugs go almost unchallenged in the ghetto where they are viciously destroying so much human potential?

5. **Welfare/Social Services** Too often our society has reduced the dignity of work to a handout.

6. **Medical** Most of the medical assistance to the poor comes in emergency situations—preventive medicine is not practiced. The family doctor is an emergency clinic.

7. **Housing** Irresponsibility of both renter and owner characterize the

total inadequacy of the housing of the poor. Meanwhile some ghettos near the cores of central cities are now becoming valuable property. Middle-class people are moving in and the poor are once again displaced.

8. **Jobs/Economic Development**   How do unskilled people find a meaningful job in a society that demands qualifications? When people are not prepared to work, a vicious cycle of dependency begins. The dollar only bounces once in the ghetto. There is no developed economy. The stores, the bars, even the dope is owned by people outside the neighborhood.

9. **Spiritual**   People need hope and faith and love. But historically this has been the task of the Church. Urban churches are understaffed and completely inundated by human need.

10. **Environment**   Dirty streets, broken mailboxes, the siren of a fire truck answering another arson call all characterize a poor neighborhood.

Research Task Force or Think Tank

The church think tank should be organized according to the ten content areas. Creative laypersons should be found and matched to their specific content area of expertise. Persons selected to work on the think tank should be comfortable handling concepts and thinking in the abstract.

Content Area	An Example of Participant
1. Education	a high school vice-principal, a teacher
2. Recreation/Culture	a director of a boys' club
3. Legal Structure	a police sergeant/a lawyer
4. Drugs/Alcohol Abuse	a church member who used to be on drugs
5. Welfare/Social Service	a social worker
6. Medical	a nurse/doctor
7. Housing	construction worker/realtor
8. Jobs/Economic Development	a personnel officer in a corporation
9. Spiritual	leader of adult Sunday school class
10. Environment	sanitation man/janitor/gardner

The Church Think Tanks Would Perform Three Functions for the Congregations

1. **Respond to Needs of Friendship Task Forces**
   As friendship task forces go to meet with the community leaders they will bring back many specific needs to which the congregations can respond. These requests should be channelled to the appropriate think tank member who has expertise in that specific matter. He will draw up

276

specific work plans to give to members of the congregation who have the abilities to implement the work plans.

2. **Build Comprehensive Work Plans**

Most of the needs of the poor can be readily anticipated: emergency food, shelter and clothing, housing, medical assistance, tutoring, drug detoxification, legal help and so on. The think tanks will develop comprehensive work plans in these areas so that almost all the needs of the poor can be responded to in an efficient and orderly way.

3. **Upgrading Creativity**

Once comprehensive work plans are developed, think tank activity should be turned toward upgrading creativity throughout the whole program. There are many people who are willing to think for the poor and there are many systems yet to be developed which could bring about extensive new assistance to the poor.

The Various Church Think Tanks Working Together

After the church think tanks have assigned ten members to take responsibility for the ten content areas, the layperson in each content area should meet with his counterparts in the other church think tanks. One of the participants would act as chairman. In this matrixed system all the housing people would meet, all the educators, all the medical people, etc., to develop the comprehensive work plans.

CHURCH THINK TANK

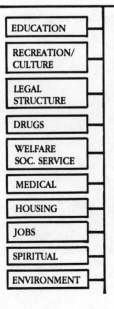

ALL THE EDUCATIONAL REPRESENTATIVES FROM THE VARIOUS CHURCH THINK TANKS WOULD MEET TOGETHER TO FORMULATE CREATIVE WORK PLANS TO SOLVE URBAN PROBLEMS.

This same process would be carried out by the other content areas. All the medical people would work together, all the housing people would work together, etc.

This would make it possible to involve many members of the congregation at the point of their skills. The work plan also brings organization of effort into all activities. The work plans would involve plans for job development, educational assistance, house renovation and ownership, preventive medicine, etc.

Seeking Creative Solutions

The church think tanks need to be constantly exploring new ideas to help the poor. Many members of the congregation can help with this search.

Church members or their friends who work in public institutions or who are educators, job developers, managers, lawyers, doctors, etc., might have valuable insights or practical solutions for helping the poor.

Corporations have developed techniques and have trained personnel who could help change institutions. A successful music company might help the music department of an urban high school, a publishing company might help the library, etc. Get the Christian community to go ask the corporations for help. Most of the corporate leaders are in the Church anyway.

Universities with their departments of Law, Education, Medicine, Architecture, Social Work, Business, have insights which have vast urban implication. Laypersons who work in colleges could become catalysts as well as students from the congregation.

Books and Periodicals can present a practical way to gather valuable insights. This is a project some retired members of the congregation might pursue.

What if, over a six-month period, selected churches from all over the country went on a creativity drive to fill national prototypes with ideas to help the poor. The creativity of the congregations would be expressed in the prototypes and then spread by the people of God to each block of each ghetto.

STEP ELEVEN   Establish think tanks in the congregations to develop work plans for the neighborhoods.

STEP ELEVEN/PART B
MORE ABOUT THINK TANKS

Hallelujah! Yes, praise the Lord! How good it is to sing his praises! How delightful, and how right!

Ps. 147:1

"good morning friends
today I do not plan
to preach a sermon
rather I want you
to preach to each other
all right everybody
stand up
I want all the educators
to meet together under the balcony
I want the medical people
to meet in the center of the sanctuary
and all the lawyers
policemen
probation officers
correction people
all of you who are part of the criminal justice system
meet in the corner over there
and all the early-child development people
all the mothers
and grandmothers
meet in that corner over there
and all the social workers
meet in the balcony
and the managers
and the salesmen
and all the youth
split up among

all the groups
they need your skills
and insights
and spirit
and everyone else
come up here
meet with me
we must decide
how to use everybody
we need to help the poor
but we can't do it just individually
we must do it together
for the next twenty minutes
I want you to talk to each other
about what you know best
what you do all day long
it's your profession
God wants your insights
He desires your skills
work hard together
as an expression of your faith
how can you take what you do
and use it
to help the poor
what is the nature of reform
how could we do it differently"
for the next twenty minutes
the sanctuary hummed
with holy activity
suggestions
creativity
long-harbored frustrations
expressed in creative specifics
about how to increase
help to the poor
at the end of the time
the leader asked his congregation
to return to their seats
and to take a few minutes
to write their ideas
on a piece of paper
then he had the choir
sing a beautiful song
while the ushers

went among the people
collecting the written expression
of their ideas for reform
the ushers brought the collection plates
to the front of the church
and the man of God
took the creativity of the people
and dedicated it to the Lord
in the name of the poor
it was a moving prayer
uttered softly
almost reverently
and the congregation said
"amen"
and left the building
feeling something profound
had just happened
but it was only
the beginning
of a whole lot more

STEP ELEVEN/PART C

THE THINK TANKS MUST DESIGN WAYS FOR THE CHURCH TO HELP THE GOVERNMENT AND THE PRIVATE SECTOR WITH SOME OF THEIR TASKS AND DEVELOP NEW EFFECTIVE PROGRAMS FOR THE CHURCH TO HELP THE POOR DIRECTLY

For Jehovah hears the cries of his needy ones, and does not look the other way.

Ps. 69:33

In the early seventies I conducted surveys in several cities to ascertain the client/staff ratio of youths, aged sixteen to twenty-one. The results showed the ratio to be seven to one. In other words, for every seven hundred youths, there were one hundred workers paid by public and private agencies to take care of their needs. But I suspect that their needs could not have been adequately met had the client/staff ratio been one to one. There were two reasons for this. First, the human resource delivery structure was fragmented. Each system was concerned with discharging its exclusive duty rather than being integrated into a functioning whole. Secondly, and even more importantly, the institutional response could not provide the kind of quality personal care so necessary to meet individual needs. Institutions are blunt instruments. They have difficulty extending the personal touch. Also, bureaucracies are too often composed of indifferent, defeated individuals.

The ghetto has many needs: education, housing, employment, health. But the greatest urban need is personalism. The desire to be known and cared about. Upon accepting the Nobel Peace Prize, Mother Teresa commented:

I have come more and more to realize that it's being unwanted that is the worst disease that any human being can ever experience.

The personal needs of the ghetto cannot be met if clients are forced to go to a number of different places to receive service. Impersonal institutions cannot satisfy deep-seated individual needs, especially when bureaucrats are so often defeated by the system.

Regardless of their imperfections, institutions must be included in any meaningful strategy which the Church develops to help the poor. On the other hand, the Church must develop its own programs to supplement existing government and private sector programs and in some cases to replace them. The existing programs by themselves have not done the job. In advancing its own program, the Church cannot afford to ignore institutions for two reasons. The first is cost. The Church simply does not have the financial resources to duplicate some services for the poor such as public education. The second reason is authority. By law, the Church cannot presume to take over courts, parks, police departments and post offices. The third reason is choice. The Church would not want to assume responsibility for such services as sanitation or replace the efforts of a private sector or government program that is working.

So the Church must have two objectives as it develops a comprehensive strategy to help the poor.

1. **The Church must assist the government's and private sector's urban efforts in all appropriate and practical ways.**

2. **The Church must develop its own programs to supplement and, in some cases, replace existing government or private sector efforts.**

A Critical Issue: The Pluralistic Contribution of the Church to Government Structures

The Church in America exists in a pluralistic society. Our nation consists of people of various religious faiths and many who profess none.

Christians understand this economically and politically. If a Christian layman is the president of a public corporation, we do not expect him to turn each management meeting into a Bible study. If he is running for political office, we do not expect him to turn each political rally into an evangelistic meeting.

While the church recognizes the ground rules of economic and political activity in a pluralistic society, it has little experience in dealing with social institutions. Some of us fight for prayer in the public schools, but we show little interest in whether or not urban public schools are teaching young students to read. Christians have a responsibility to assist the government and private sector in its efforts to help the poor.

We must remember that these structures are pluralistic and therefore not an arena for our evangelism. Instead, they should be the objects of our concerned service. The government and the private sector must intensify the quality of its assistance to the poor and the Christian community must mobilize its resources to help them.

Think Tank convenes to attempt to solve an urban problem

STEP TWELVE/PART A

DEVELOP SKILLS TASK FORCE TO APPLY THE SKILLS OF THE CONGREGATION TO THE NEEDS OF THE POOR

These things I have told you are all true. Insist on them so that Christians will be careful to do good deeds all the time, for this is not only right but it brings results.

Titus 3:8

The function of the skills task force is to take the abilities of the congregation and direct them to the needs of the poor. This cannot be done without careful management.

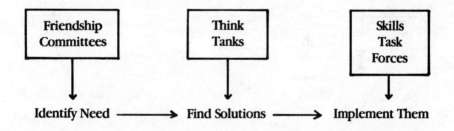

An Example:

| Friendship Committee | Meets with a Junior High School principal. He wants some computers for the students in his school. |

| Think Tank | Decides that help can best be given to the principal by showing him how to solve his own need. A skills task force would be instructed to help the principal draw up a proposal for presentation to corporations and appointments would be secured for him. |

Skills Task Force	A small group of laypersons help the principal draw up an effective proposal explaining the need for computers in the school. They also come up with a list of contacts highly-placed in the business community. Eventually, five corporation presidents or vice presidents are targeted and appointments are made.

The principal received his computers.

In many respects the skills task forces are the pivitol part of the program. Without their abilities we could not satisfy the requests of the institutional leaders and public servants. Without their input we could not deliver specific resources to the individual families with whom the ministry teams will be working. The activities of the skills task force are crucial. They are the axle that turns the wheel.

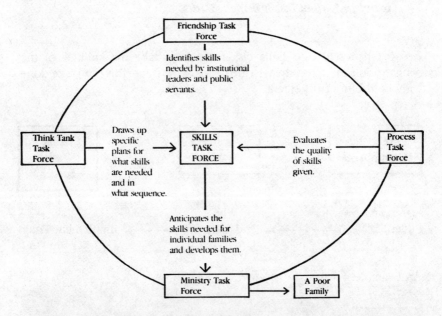

The reason why it is so difficult for the laypersons in the congregations to give their skills to the needs of the poor is because there has been no structure for the exchange. The friendship, ministry, process task forces and the think tanks provide this mechanism in the form of a matrix or grid. The friendship teams identify institutional needs, the think tanks translate those needs into designated skills and construct plans for their implementation. The ministry teams help to pave the way for those skills to be delivered to individual families and the process task forces maintain quality control of all efforts.

Some critics might suggest that this is all too complicated. But the alternative is what we have now—churches filled with skills and ghettos filled with needs. Skills need to operate within a structure to be effective. The task forces provide that structure.

STEP TWELVE   Develop skills task forces to apply the skills of the congregation to meet the needs of the poor.

Bringing tutoring skills to school

STEP TWELVE / PART B
SOME PRACTICAL USES OF SKILLS

Education

- Tutor a youngster.

- Help to revamp a data processing system in a welfare office or school system.

- Help to redesign a remedial system for the fourth graders of an inner-city school.

- Help to upgrade the nutritional value of the food served in an inner-city high school.

- Give some inner-city youth swimming lessons.

- Teach some inner-city youth about opening up a bank account and how to balance a checkbook.

- Volunteer to help in an inner-city day-care center.

- Give some unused musical instruments out of some suburban attics and into an inner-city school.

- Donate some meaningful books to an inner-city library.

- Give inner-city students a tour of your factory or corporation.

- Allow a principal to go on a management training program with some of your corporate managers.

- Conduct a language class for some Hispanic mothers.

- Build an ad campaign for not dropping out of school.

- If you have a son or daughter in a college, take a couple of junior high school students along. It might inspire them to go, too.

- Give technical assistance to the design of a year book.

- Help an inner-city youth fill out properly his scholarship and loan program for college.

- Take an inner-city kid to the library and find out from the microfilm newspapers what was happening in the world the day the youth was born.

- Get twenty kids an appointment to see the mayor.

- Develop a program for encouraging and developing exceptional art skills.

- Develop some effective sex education.

Legal

- Assist a probation officer with his caseload.

- Lawyers giving legal assistance to inner-city need are always needed.

Recreation/Culture

- Take some youth on a weekend trip.

- Organize a Boy Scout troop for an inner-city church.

- Sponsor trophies for an inner-city basketball tournament.

- Help to start a garden in the ghetto.

- Take some inner-city kids on a ride in a private airplane.

- Talk to some inner-city landlords about keeping up their homes better for their tenants.

- Take some students to a professional baseball game.

- Sponsor a youth to go to a Christian camp in the summer.

- Encourage some senior citizens to spend time with young inner-city children.

- Encourage and teach some inner-city youth to start a stamp collection.

- Have an inner-city family share their culture with you and begin a relationship.

- Go and take some pictures of some inner-city kids and talk to them about Christ.

- Get an inner-city grade school teacher twenty pumpkins to give away for Halloween.

- Get some famous people or athletes to sign personalized autographs.

- Help start a weight-loss class in the ghetto.

Drugs

- Meet with the chief of police and offer to help him on some problems he can identify as needing help.

- Have a group of lawyers talk with some drug addicts and get their insights about how drugs are brought into the community. Then do something about their insights.

- Make available your company's alcoholic program for some policemen who might have the same problem.

Jobs

- Find someone a job.

- Assist some new employee from the ghetto who has just begun to work for your company and become a mentor to that person for the next few years.

- Give an inner-city student a part-time job after school.

- Help to start meaningful small businesses in the ghetto.

- Give technical assistance in accounting to inner-city group.

- Give management skills to assist in getting the government out of the welfare business.

Housing

- As a plumber or carpenter take your skill to assist an inner-city dweller.

- Help to design a financial system so inner-city dwellers can own their own homes.

Spiritual

- Help to lead a Bible study for an inner-city church.

- If your youth group has an extra good program, invite an inner-city youth group to join you.

- One of the most important ways to help respond to spiritual need is to encourage your church to sponsor an inner-city church. Most inner-city churches have a pastor who does everything and no staff.

- Book a black choir to sing in some white churches.

- Get youth tickets to Christian musicals or to attend events in your church.

Health

- Volunteer to provide medical services.

- Volunteer to spend some time in the waiting room of an inner-city hospital.

- Begin or participate in a clinic to help insure that every inner-city youth has his teeth examined twice a year.

- Make sure every kid has an eye exam.

Environment

- Have someone figure out where you put what you want to throw away on an inner-city street where there are no garbage containers because they have been stolen.

STEP THIRTEEN/PART A

DEVELOP MINISTRY TEAMS TO MEET THE TOTAL NEEDS OF POOR FAMILIES

> If there is a poor man among your brothers in any of the towns of the land that the Lord your God is giving you, do not be hardhearted or tightfisted toward your poor brother. Rather be openhanded and freely lend him whatever he needs.
>
> Deut. 15:7-11

One of the major reasons for our continuous failure in American ghettos is that we have not tried to solve all the problems of poor people all at once. So much urban help has been one-dimensional. We have found someone a job, or gotten them a lawyer, or tutored their children, or found them an apartment, or secured them medical assistance, or financial assistance, or provided them food stamps. Instead of getting someone everything, we have gotten him something. Our efforts have amounted to stopgap measures, and these tend to unravel quickly. People need all their basic needs met to function properly. Food without shelter leaves you cold. Shelter without food leaves you hungry. And food and shelter without clothes leave you naked. We cannot continue to pursue piecemeal strategies if we wish to succeed.

Another important reason the government has failed so desperately in the ghetto is that it could not provide for the spiritual needs of the poor. Of course, that was not the government's or private sector's responsibility but the Church's. Welfare, drug abuse, abandoned families, crime, etc., are fundamentally spiritual problems that demand spiritual solutions. Government efforts would have been more successful had the Church not abandoned the ghetto.

All strategies for helping the poor must have one bottom line: effective delivery of services to meet individual needs. Our society has appropriated enough resources to help its poor but it has failed to design effective systems to deliver them. Most of what we attempted to give never arrived.

But even the Great Society's staunchest defenders admit that the cost of its success has been high. Many of its programs were not

293

well thought out; others were ravaged by Congress through compromise and unholy alliance, resulting in high levels of fraud and mismanagement. By some estimates, for every dollar spent on the war on poverty today only ten cents ever directly reaches the poor.

Newsweek; April 5, 1982

The actual delivery of help is every bit as important as appropriating the resources in the first place. How can the Church succeed in an area where so many have failed? The Church must help to (1) build effective programs to help the poor, and (2) deliver them successfully to individual families.

It is the latter capacity that ministry teams have been expressly created to serve.

1. Building Effective Programs

Quality programs can be designed through the church think tank. Up until now I have emphasized the role of task forces in helping *institutions* help the poor. Their relationship can be charted in the following way:

The Church Serving Institutions

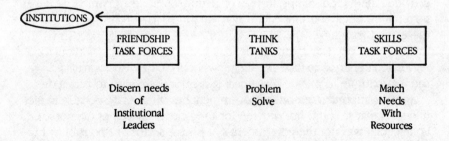

But the think tanks and skills task forces must also serve the ministry teams as they concentrate upon individual poor persons and families. Public institutions and private agencies cannot meet all the needs of an urban family. Church members working on ministry teams are in an ideal position to support them by providing needed caring and personalism. Think tanks help ministry teams to help families in the following way:

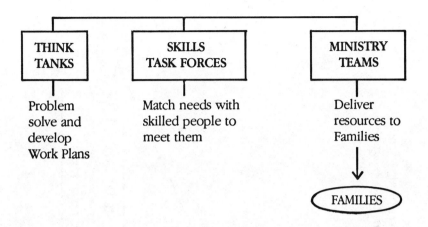

The think tank must develop work plans for all areas of family need: education, recreational and cultural activities, jobs/economic development, housing, criminal justice structures, medical assistance, drug and alcohol abuse, welfare/social services, spiritual and the environment. The solutions think tanks construct for ministry teams need not necessarily be novel ones; they simply need to be efficient and workable. Often this may involve repackaging existing ideas and structures.

A work plan to address typical urban education problems, for example, might aim to involve thousands of volunteers from the congregations who might affect students in the following ways:

(1) **supplement classroom instruction with special presentations.**
Example—a computer demonstration for the students; thirty pumpkins for Halloween with a related historical and botany lesson; arranging to bring a well-known personality into the classroom.

(2) **provide seminars to supplement curriculum**
Example—field trips to cultural activities, seminars of various hobbies people have developed, field trips to their work place.

(3) **develop independent study projects**
Example—an analysis of how a firehouse is organized; a study on how a college recruits football players, a survey on how the criminal justice system is organized (these independent study projects are supervised by concerned laypersons).

(4) **coordinate tutorial assistance**
Example—supplying tutors for the four children of Mrs. Jennie Smith, a welfare client whose children are many years behind in reading level.

FULL FLOW CHART OF ACTIVITIES

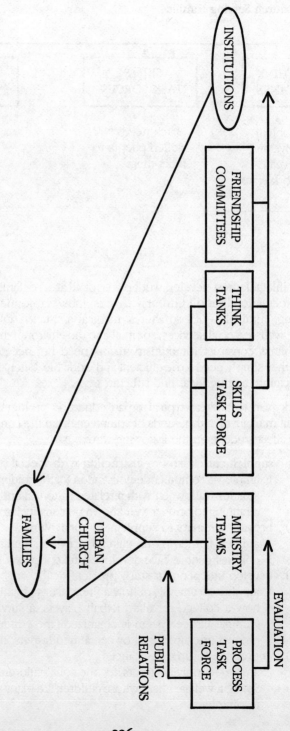

The think tanks and the skill committees serve both the friendship committees and the ministry teams. Friendship committees serve institutions. Ministry teams serve families. The process task force evaluates the effectiveness of all activities.

296

2. SUCCESSFULLY DELIVERING EFFECTIVE PROGRAMS TO INDIVID-
   UAL POOR FAMILIES
   a. Develop Personal Inventory Teams
   This function is crucial. You can develop a lifesaving medicine, but it
   must be injected into the blood stream to be effective. You can find a
   donor of a human organ, but it must be transferred without the new
   body rejecting it. Work plans and ambitious schemes are fine, but the
   successful transfer of resources to an individual poor person on a run-
   down street in a ghetto is the critical test of a program.

   Resources cannot be transferred until the needs of individual families
   have been assessed. This could be accomplished by a team of
   laypersons trained to diagnose family needs in terms of the ten
   content areas. The team should not consist of more than five persons
   so it would be necessary to compress the ten areas of urban need
   into five composite functions. Each function could become the
   responsibility of a layperson from the church who has professional
   expertise in that area.

WORK PLAN	COMPOSITE FUNCTION
1. EDUCATION RECREATION/CULTURE	EDUCATION
2. JOBS	JOBS
3. WELFARE/SOCIAL SERVICE LEGAL STRUCTURES MEDICAL DRUGS	SOCIAL SERVICE
4. HOUSING ENVIRONMENT	FINANCIAL MANAGEMENT
5. SPIRITUAL	SPIRITUAL

b. Diagnose the Comprehensive Needs of a Poor Family

Personal inventory teams from the church congregations would meet with a poor family to ascertain their total needs. Some might fear that five-member teams might be over-kill. However, I doubt if too much of the right kind of attention can be given over a short period of time. Also, the teams will be dealing with very difficult problems that demand expertise and sensitivity beyond the scope of a single individual. Finally, laypersons are very busy. The team must be large enough so that if one or two members cannot participate on a visit, the remaining members can perform its function.

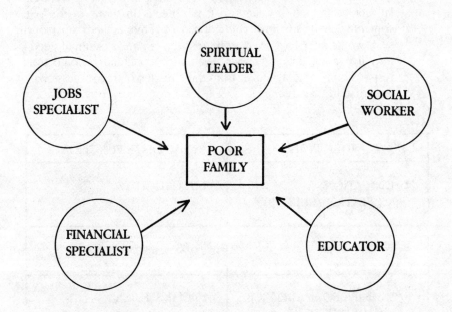

The personal inventory team members will conduct a series of interviews and tests in order to identify the comprehensive needs of the family.

- the reading levels of all members of the family would be measured

- plans would be developed to provide cultural and recreational opportunities

- tutorial programs would be devised for each child as necessary

- early child development programs would be explored

- extensive vocational testing would be conducted to discover abilities and interests

- transportation needs would be identified and adequately provided for
- child care opportunities would be explored
- thorough medical exams would be given
- nutritional needs would be looked into
- drug and alcohol abuse problems would be treated
- job opportunities would be presented
- dental exams would be conducted
- counseling would be arranged if needed
- any legal needs would be addressed
- special programs would be available for anyone pregnant or incarcerated
- housing needs would be assessed and alternatives developed
- social service needs would be explored
- financial planning would be offered
- spiritual assistance would be offered
- and the list would go on

The personal inventory team would complete their task by writing prescriptions for the family in all areas of their lives. These prescriptions would draw upon the work plans created by the think tanks. All prescriptions would be established on a quid pro quo basis (if we/then you; e.g., if we secure a loan, then you must pay it back. If we provide the tutor, then you enforce study time.)

The personal inventory teams would not continue to help the family. After recording their prescriptions, they would move on to the next family.

c. **Ministry Teams to Individual Families**

This becomes the heart of the program. All efforts lead to this specific activity. Two couples are selected to work with a poor family. One of the two couples should be the same ethnic background of the family. This two-couple ministry team would work with the poor family until all prescriptions have been implemented and a climate of advantage created. This could involve several years of participation.

Some may decry these ministry teams as paternalistic. However, it is not what you do that makes you paternalistic, but how you do it. If the ministry teams come as servants, they will be welcomed as friends and their assistance will be received gratefully. Besides, the help given according to this plan would also make demands upon the recipients. This would further protect against the development of unhealthy attitudes.

All assistance given to the poor families must be given in the name of Christ. It may not always be received that way. But the task of the Church is to share the love and message of Christ. The results are left in God's hands. Christian families should be helped first and then attempts should be made to help everyone.

Once a family has made significant progress, the ministry team can move on to another family. In this way the Church would be helping to solve a problem and not simply to contain one. Also, once a family has been helped, it may be in a position to help other families. Welfare and handouts usually produce more welfare and handouts, but families who receive meaningful help can now generate positive momentum. When hundreds of families climb out of poverty and begin to help hundreds of other families get out of poverty, a movement has begun. The Church has the capacity to start and sustain such a movement.

The poverty problem in our country would be confined to those who won't or can't work. As for those who won't, there is little we can do and for those who can't, there should be no limit to both our compassion and our resources.

The Family Ministry Task Force should function as follows:

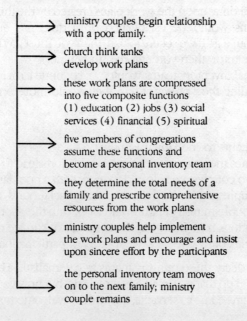

ministry couples begin relationship
with a poor family.

church think tanks
develop work plans

these work plans are compressed
into five composite functions
(1) education (2) jobs (3) social
services (4) financial (5) spiritual

five members of congregations
assume these functions and
become a personal inventory team

they determine the total needs of a
family and prescribe comprehensive
resources from the work plans

ministry couples help implement
the work plans and encourage and insist
upon sincere effort by the participants

the personal inventory team moves
on to the next family; ministry
couple remains

The personal inventory teams and ministry teams are the crucial and unique part of this specific plan. Their activities could bring help to every poor person in America who wants to help himself and his family. It provides the church with a plausable plan to assist self sufficiency of the citizen of the ghetto.

Some observations on personal inventory and ministry teams:

1. Only help familys that ask for help and one willing to work hard to receive the help.
2. Only continue help if there is reasonable response.
3. Ministry teams should spend short times relating to families before the personal inventory teams are brought in.
4. The personal inventory teams are the managers of the ministry teams and provide additional help as new problems and opportunities arise.
5. The personal inventory teams cannot handle more than 10-15 ministry teams. As a program grows in a church additional personal inventory teams would have to be created.

STEP THIRTEEN Develop ministry teams to meet the total needs of poor families.

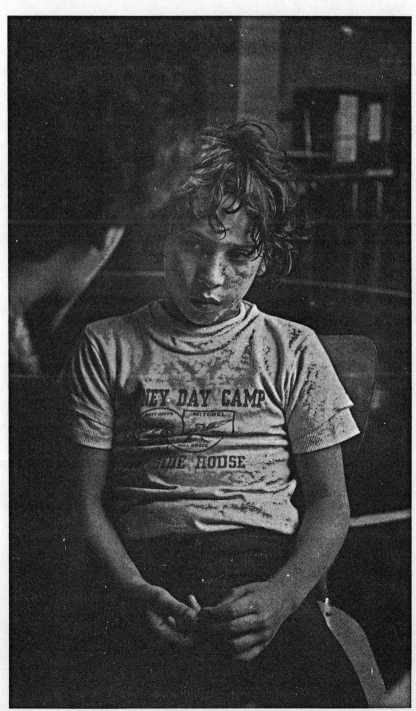

A Ministry Team Member in action

STEP THIRTEEN/PART B

AN EXAMPLE OF HELP TO A POOR FAMILY

Mrs. Sally Smith was on welfare. She had five children ages three, seven, ten, fourteen and sixteen. She had a man who had been staying with her off and on for five years and was the father of her youngest child. They all lived in a small, run-down house across the street from the housing project. One Sunday a neighbor took Sally Smith to the First Urban Church and she became a Christian. Rev. Jones arranged for a personal inventory team and ministry couples to work with Mrs. Smith and her family. The appointment was made for Tuesday night at 7:30.

A ministry team from the First Christian Church came to meet with Mrs. Smith and her family. The meeting lasted two hours and the ground rules were laid out:

1.   The whole family would work together on solving their problems, acknowledging that their difficulties were interrelated.

2.   Jesus Christ was the reason the group had been formed, his help was essential.

3.   Hard work would be needed. There would be no handouts. If people didn't work to solve the problems, they would be dropped from the program.

4.   Comprehensive solutions would be sought after.

5.   The ministry team would stay with the family as long as it took to bring comprehensive and lasting help.

For the next month the five-member personal inventory team worked with the Sally Smith family. Edna Clark, the educator, tested Mrs. Smith and each of the children. The team recommended that the three-year-old Smith child begin attending the new Christian day care center that had been established in the neighborhood. She would receive educational enrichment in preparation for entering formal school in two years. The seven, ten and fourteen-year-old children were found to be far below normal in math and reading levels. Edna visited all their teachers and they were put into extensive tutorial programs with volunteers. Mrs. Smith promised to enforce evening and weekend study times. The sixteen-year-old Smith boy was essentially a dropout. Although in the ninth grade, he tested at the fourth grade reading level. As he would be seventeen the following week, he was placed in a neighborhood church street academy recently established for dropouts. Mrs. Smith herself had received little formal education and was virtually illiterate. She was enrolled in special adult educational programs which had been started in the community.

Herbert Wellington, the person on the personal inventory team, talked with Mrs. Smith about the financial and housing situation of the family. It could be described in one word: terrible. Mr. Wellington recommended to Mrs. Smith an immediate move as the rent was exorbitant and the facilities almost beyond repair. Within two days the family moved to a nicer and cheaper house three blocks away with the help of a skills task force. Mr. Wellington also promised that if Mrs. Smith was faithful in carrying out all the recommendations of the inventory team, within a year, home ownership would be discussed. This would fulfill a dream Mrs. Smith had always had.

Elizabeth Clover was the social worker on the personal inventory team. She had medical and dental tests performed on the whole family. Assorted medical problems emerged and extensive dental work was required. The older Smith boy had a case pending in the courts and was already on probation. Ms. Clover gave the case to a Christian lawyer. The boy also admitted that he had a drug problem. He was assigned to a new drug clinic that the church had just opened in the neighborhood. The 10-year-old Smith girl was very withdrawn. She was introduced to a volunteer from one of the churches who was gifted in counseling younger children.

There were two additional problems that Elizabeth had to deal with. One was that Mrs. Smith was presently on welfare. Elizabeth didn't recommend she go off welfare immediately. She did not have the skill to find employment which matched her present compensation and she had five children to feed. But Elizabeth Clover did insist that Mrs. Smith begin to play a more active role in raising her children. The past had been handled irresponsibly. In addition Elizabeth wanted Mrs. Smith to begin to upgrade her skills and prepare for eventual participation in the world of work.

The second problem was Mrs. Smith's man, Edward Dole. They had an unofficial-official relationship. But because of welfare regulations they were living a deception. Mrs. Smith's youngest child had been by him and the two had a fairly healthy relationship despite the handicaps. But the Christian moral and legal implications had to be dealt with. Elizabeth assigned them to a black counselor from one of the churches to begin long-term resolution.

Felix Edwards was the jobs person on the personal inventory team. He gave vocational tests to Mrs. Smith and her eldest son. He also gave tests to Edward Dole. All three were placed in training programs reflecting their vocational interests. Mrs. Smith's oldest son was placed in a part-time job and Edward Dole received a full-time one. Both jobs had been developed by a church skills task force.

Henry Oliver was the spiritual person on the personal inventory team. He arranged for Mrs. Smith to enter a new discipleship course at church. Edward Dole agreed to participate in class to understand more about the Christian faith. So did Mrs. Smith's oldest child. The three younger children were enrolled in a Christian education class.

After several weeks the members of the personal inventory team wrote comprehensive prescriptions for all areas of the needs of the Smith family. The ministry couples assumed all responsibility for implementing the prescriptions of the personal inventory teams.

Within a year great changes have occurred in the Smith family. The most significant is that Mrs. Smith has gotten married to Edward Dole. She now has a part-time job and is off welfare. Edward Dole is doing well in his job and has received a promotion. The oldest son is drug-free and doing fine in the street academy. Within another year he will graduate and wants to pursue a career in the army. His case has been dropped by the courts. Some progress has been demonstrated by all the younger children. The family is active in the church and a triumphant story is emerging. Within six months the ministry couples will leave the Smith's and go on to serve their next family.

STEP FOURTEEN

DEVELOP A PROCESS COMMITTEE FOR EVALUATION AND PUBLIC RELATIONS

A dull axe requires great strength; be wise and sharpen the blade.

Eccles. 10:10

No management task is complete without an evaluation function. Goals must be set. But goals must also be met.

Any congregation has laypersons with the skills to measure the performance of help given to the poor. Perhaps the best candidate for this function would be the professional analyst who daily monitors his company's progress.

It would be useful if the process committee also takes on the public relations function. Most churches have a place where the coffee is served every Sunday. A timely display would be in order. Bulletin inserts would capture interest while well-designed newsletters could chart the progress of the church program.

People come to church each Sunday to be spiritually challenged and to worship God. But most members also want to give God the skills that they have. The process task force gives some of the members of the congregations a chance to use their analytical and public relations skills to help the poor.

STEP FOURTEEN   Develop a process committee for evaluation and public relations.

306

STEP FIFTEEN

TRAIN VOLUNTEERS TO MANAGE THE PROGRAM

In the city of Joppa there was a woman called Dorcas, a believer who is always doing kind things for others, especially for the poor.

Acts 9:36

Programs are only as successful as the people who organize and run them. Yet professional staff people must be paid a fair wage if they are to devote their full time to serving others. Many well-designed public and private programs have been crippled because of this expensive reality.

The church strategy outlined here has, therefore, been structured with history and economy in mind. To this point, every step of the program has required total volunteer help outside of the paid church staff. Yet this phase of the strategy introduces a special task force of individuals with even more substantial amounts of time to lend to crucial management functions.

Acts 9:36 focused on a woman called Dorcas who exemplified the concept of constant service. In every American city there are significant numbers of women, retired folks, and men who have the time and talent available to do the same. Some women have raised children to maturity and are looking for a challengeing new way to give of themselves. Others were once in the business or education worlds before starting families and have grown bored with conventional club and charity involvements. Furthermore, many men and women have retired from executive positions, but do not wish to set aside the challenges of management totally.

To this pool of highly skilled individuals, the program offers special Dorcas-like responsibilities such as the following:

- Dorcas persons surround each church chairman or task force chairman with volunteers who would have the time and ability to perform many administrative and coordinating functions.

- Dorcas persons would make sure that all friendship committee members are informed of next meeting, see that all requests for help are funnelled to proper think tank, and keep tabs on the progress of all solutions.

- Dorcas persons would screen all requests to the think tank, bring solution to the simpler ones, help with the development of work plans, and facilitate communication to both friendship committees and skill groups.

- Dorcas persons would help skill chairman organize skill teams, implement their tasks and coordinate their results.

- Dorcas persons would provide background material for ministry couples, help to place them with their families, assist personal inventory teams with support services and help urban pastors with program development.

- Dorcas persons would provide assistance for process chairmen for the development of evaluation and public relations program.

STEP FIFTEEN **Train volunteers to manage the program.**

STEP SIXTEEN

DEVELOP SPIRITUAL MINISTRIES IN THE NEIGHBORHOOD

. . . See I have placed before you an open door . . .

Rev. 3:8

Why neighborhoods are so important to the development of urban churches:

Neighborhoods play an important part in the life of most poor folk. This is not true of more affluent people. In most suburban communities and apartment complexes people hardly know their neighbors.

However, inner-city neighborhoods have closer communication. More people are squeezed into less real estate. In the warmer weather people take to the streets and spend endless hours "hanging out." Many unemployed people spend their time sitting around a given block. Few people have cars. Some almost never leave the neighborhood. All of these factors make for heightened interaction between local folk.

Folks from suburbia seldom select a church on the basis of neighborhood. Usually, they are attracted by a choir, a preacher, friends, prestige, denomination, or some other factor. If they have to travel several extra miles to find what they want, they are not greatly inconvenienced.

People from poor areas respond best to local churches. But most of the churches now in their neighborhoods are filled with middle-class people who drive in each Sunday. Consequently, they aren't comfortable there. If six or more pastors were ever put on the staff of a church in a poor neighborhood and a forum was created to express the needs of the poor, that church would be packed out all week long.

What should an urban church focused upon a poor neighborhood look like?

The Staff The staff of six to twelve pastors would be freed all day to minister to the people of the neighborhood. Like the apostles, they would be available to teach, to preach, and to pray. The staff would begin its day with collective prayer and spiritual discipline in order to

309

promote internal health and strength. Then they would go out among the people all day long: loving all they encountered, responding to requests for help, visiting the sick and imprisoned, teaching Bible studies, instructing new converts in their faith, and sharing Christ's Gospel. Their salaries would be provided by the suburban churches.

The Building The church building probably should resemble a large living room with a carpet and lots of little corners where people can talk in small groups with the pastors and among themselves. A large storefront or even a large apartment would be more than adequate for a beginning. There should be little that could be stolen. It could have a small chapel but a sanctuary is not needed. A local school or hall could be rented for Sunday use. The church building should be open twenty-four hours a day, seven days a week and always have someone there who cares. Whenever a person has a problem, or just needs to be near someone, he can run over to the building. The building would become the hub for many activities.

The Work **Equipping the Saints** Any urban neighborhood is filled with Christians. But most of these disciples have never been given quality spiritual instruction and help. This is a great indictment on the Christian community. The seeds of renewal in any urban neighborhood are in place. They have just never been developed. This must become the first task of the urban church.

Organizing Blocks Bible studies, prayer groups, leadership training can be developed on each block. The blocks or housing project units provide the natural strategy for organization.

Disbursement of Resources This task is carried out by the local urban church members and the suburban church task forces. The urban pastors should be freed from all responsibilities of resource procurement. As in the early church, the deacons should meet the physical needs freeing the pastors for spiritual ministries.

Changing the Neighborhood One of the results of the activities of the people of God in the neighborhood must become comprehensive change that will affect the physical appearance and the delivery of human services. Drugs must be driven out. Crime must be challenged. Housing must be renovated. Schools must be improved and so on.

At the risk of repetition, I would like to summarize my strategy for the urban church. The best way to reach poor folks is to create something just for them. The music, the preaching, the programs, the building should be geared directly to their needs. They must not be fit into an existing program or made to conform to be accepted. Very few middle-class or affluent churches, black, white, or Hispanic, can make these adjustments. Therefore, very few middle-class or affluent churches, black, white, or Hispanic, should make those adjustments. Middle-class and affluent churches have legitimate needs to be met in their own congregations. Their preaching, music, program must reflect that.

Furthermore, ministering to the poor would mean enormous security problems. A ghetto church will be robbed over and over again. There will be wine bottles left in the building, unflushed toilets, incredible wear and tear on the building, untimely disruptions in the service, physical danger to staff, and some church members' children may be exposed to drugs and negative influences. This is a price few middle-class churches can, or perhaps, should absorb without damaging their existing ministries.

The logical solution, then, is to create well-staffed and supplied urban spiritual centers which can reach out to the poor with programs just for them. The middle-class congregations can channel their supplies and manpower through these centers.

Indigenous leadership can be developed in these new urban churches. Potential leaders already exist in the blocks of our poor neighborhoods. There are many Christians who have prayed for years that God would come help their block. They have only awaited the creation of structures and resources to which they could give their leadership. Also, as God touches many people in the neighborhood and they respond, new sources of street leadership will emerge. When these folks reach spiritual maturity, no urban block will ever be the same.

One last comment. Some middle-class and affluent churches conduct unusual ministries to the poor and some congregations have unusual economic and racial diversity among their membership. Some of these situations are the result of a highly gifted pastor or unusual commitment by groups of laypersons. Most of these diversified congregations took years to build and incredible efforts to maintain. These churches deserve to be applauded and represent exciting examples of what needs to be duplicated throughout church-life in America. However, the necessity for speed and the reality of asking whole congregations to shift directions dictates that new churches be developed just for the poor. This is obviously not the New Testament example. But I don't think poor people should have to wait for that to happen to get the kind of help they need.

America must break out of its poverty cycle. Our spiritual health depends on it, as does our social and economic well-being. Too often the Church has avoided responsibility. The salt of the earth has had little to pour. The light of the world has been trapped in its own darkness. At the point of greatest need, we expended the least and expected it to be an expression of our faith. And perhaps, tragically, this is the case. We must give the urban church more to work with.

STEP SIXTEEN **Develop spiritual ministries in the neighborhood.**

STEP SIXTEEN/PART B

AN EXAMPLE OF AN EFFECTIVE URBAN CHURCH IN ACTION

The First Urban Church has a senior pastor and a staff of ten ministers. Its parish is a poor neighborhood measuring twenty blocks which includes a large housing project. The area is almost completely black (although it could have been Hispanic or another minority). Rev. Tom Jones is the senior pastor. There are three other churches in the neighborhood. Two of them consist primarily of people who no longer live in the neighborhood. A third is a small storefront church but it is exerting little impact.

The first day Rev. Jones started the ministry he was overwhelmed by the openness of the people. Everyone accepted him. As Rev. Jones began to work his blocks it became increasingly evident that no one from the church was around. The plan called for one new staff member a month for ten months until the full complement was on board.

The building Rev. Jones secured for the church was an old furniture store that had been vacant for two years. After ten months the staffing was complete. Rev. Jones filled the staff positions after the skill areas of the think tank.

Minister one—had educational skills
Minister two—had recreational and cultural skills
Minister three—had job development skills
Minister four—had construction experience
Minister five—had counseling skills
Minister six—had legal skills
Minister seven—had medical skills
Minister eight—had substance abuse skills
Minister nine—had exceptional Bible teaching skills
Minister ten—had great interest in landscaping

Seven of the ministers were black, two were white and one Hispanic. One was female. Half were married. All lived in the neighborhood.

The day started at 8:30 with an hour and a half meeting. There was a common meal and a spiritual time. No business was discussed. It was an attempt to provide spiritual vitality and protect against conflicts and emotional burnout. The rest of the day the ministers gave themselves to the people in the neighborhood. They maintained a constant presence. They were involved. They were everywhere.

Their first task was to identify all the Christians in the neighborhood and begin to build them up in their faith. They organized them by blocks of buildings in the housing projects. Each group had a leader. All the leaders gathered together once a week. No minister spent any time procuring resources for the needs of the neighborhood. This was done by the congregations of the five suburban churches who had agreed to help the neighborhood. These needs were identified and coordinated by the block leaders.

There was always a minister in the church building 16 hours a day. Various block leaders also took turns manning the building. The church became the center of the neighborhood. Each minister was responsible for a specific block and its leaders. Each minister also had a skill area. All ministers were required to leave the neighborhood two days a week to protect against burnout.

Various pastors were assigned program development areas. A vital senior adult program had been formed to minister to their needs and use their skills to help others. Spiritual discipleship training was everywhere. There was constant outreach initiatives by both laypersons and pastors to every aspect of the community. All the social needs of the neighborhood were being addressed. A strong youth program had been developed. Aggressive day care and Christian education programs were flourishing. Community structures had been organized to insure long-term revitalization of the area.

On Sunday, the church rented the auditorium of the local school. Although the church was only 10 months old it was already packing out all available seats. One-seventh of the neighborhood was now going to church. But church was now happening all week long. The Church of Jesus Christ had come to the neighborhood.

STEP SEVENTEEN

DEVELOP SPECIFIC PROGRAMS IN THE DESIGNATED NEIGHBORHOOD

Most individuals live in families and urban families live in neighborhoods. Helping poor people involves helping them as individuals, as families, and as neighborhoods. Our efforts at all three levels must interrelate.

When we strengthen the parts of the neighborhood we strengthen the whole. The think tank is responsible for designing plans to upgrade the parts of the neighborhood. These plans will be based largely on the requests of institutional leaders as conveyed to the various friendship task forces. Without strengthening the neighborhood we will have great difficulty meeting the needs of families and individuals.

I suggest that four areas of the neighborhood deserve special concentration. These are: (1) content, (2) coordination, (3) community involvement, and (4) spiritual.

1. Content

Creative ideas can be implemented in all neighborhoods in a multitude of areas. The education process can be greatly enhanced. Volunteers could help teachers directly in classrooms by providing the manpower to lead separate reading groups, work with slow learners, accompany teachers on field trips, and instruct children in games and related physical education activities. In addition, volunteers could operate afternoon tutorials and weekend independent study projects designed to complement the classroom curriculum. Volunteers with medical skills could set up health clinics using neighborhood people as staff. Crime watch programs could be instituted and proper rapport with police established. Volunteers with legal skills could exercise their imaginations to give constructive assistance to courts and probation officers. Job development, job training, and career counseling could all be begun and operated by volunteers. Prevention and rehabilitation programs could be created to deal with the severe drug abuse and alcohol problems. Beautification of any neighborhood can be accomplished by concerned citizens working along with and providing incentives for neighborhood folk. Volunteers could make important inroads into the welfare problem by giving instruction in effective parenting. Urban churches could be better staffed to promote the spiritual vitality of neighborhoods.

2. Coodination

We must restructure much of the human service delivery system.

TRADITIONAL SERVICE DELIVERY SYSTEM

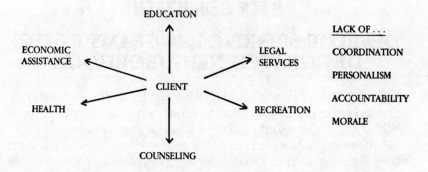

What is needed is a new marketing plan. The present approach is to ask the client to find the resource. We must create systems in which the resources find the client. We must change the direction of the arrows.

PROPOSED SERVICE DELIVERY SYSTEM

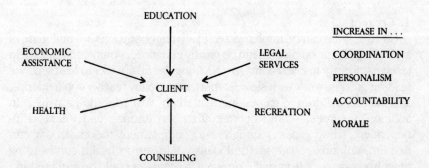

3. Community Involvement

Longlasting urban change must involve and eventually emanate from the people in the neighborhood. It cannot be imposed and sustained from without. This is one of the three premises of the program. You must work with the together people within the neighborhoods to bring about change. But those folks must be better equipped and supported.

4. Spiritual

You cannot change a hurting neighborhood without speaking to the spirit of the people. We must strengthen the inner-city Church.

The most effective way to change a neighborhood is to strengthen individual parts. When you improve the parts you improve the whole. It becomes the task of the think tanks to develop plans for upgrading all activities and of skill task forces to implement those plans.

STEP SEVENTEEN   Develop specific programs in the designated neighborhood.

STEP EIGHTEEN

REPLICATE THE RESULTS OF INITIAL PROTOTYPE INTO OTHER POOR NEIGHBORHOODS OF THE CITY

Two can accomplish more than twice as much as one, for the results can be much better.

Eccles. 4:9

Once four to seven churches have produced a functioning prototype in a neighborhood of their city, they can consider reproducing it elsewhere. At this point, much of the difficult tactical work and organization has been done. Momentum has been established. Success has been accomplished. Experience has been gained.

A functioning prototype has two principle merits. First, it silences critics and skeptics who believed it could not be done. Secondly, it provides a working visual aid with which to explain the program to people who have difficulty understanding it on paper.

At this point, the successful churches have many options in replicating the prototype. Each of the participating churches can gather new partners and start in several new neighborhoods at once. Or, the original churches can stay together and encourage other congregations to follow their example. Or, they can pursue a combination of both approaches. The final plans that are agreed upon must be well organized and patiently managed. It will take years of sustained effort to turn around whole neighborhoods.

I have one further comment. The four to seven churches working together in a specific neighborhood become the basic unit of work. They act as a self-contained entity. This is sound management for several reasons. First, a self-contained unit provides durability. Poor people need relationships sustained over a long period of time. Second, it provides internal strength which is not easily corrupted by city-wide personality conflicts and the inevitable turf battles that develop even among Christians. Finally, a self-contained unit promotes internal consistency and this enhances the church's ability to get things done rapidly and in coordinated fashion.

STEP EIGHTEEN   Reproduce the results of the original prototype to other poor neighborhoods.

STEP NINETEEN

ORGANIZE A CITY COMMITTEE FOR RESTRUCTURING THE HUMAN SERVICE DELIVERY SYSTEM

There is a time for everything
A time to tear;
A time to repair:

Eccles. 3:7

The relationship between any ghetto neighborhood and the rest of the city must be considered by church planners in helping the poor. A public school is legally related to the City Board of Education and the school principal must report to somebody downtown. Likewise, the policeman on the corner reports to a sergeant at headquarters and the social worker handling the local welfare caseload reports to a superior outside the neighborhood. Sooner or later, if you are going to take quality help to an urban neighborhood, you have to deal with city-wide human service delivery systems and political structures.

Federal, state, and county programs as well as organizations with city-wide impact, such as United Way and Chamber of Commerce, must be dealt with on a city-wide basis. Groups like the Council of Churches, Salvation Army, and Boy's Club often have many locations, projects or related groups in a city. It is necessary to work with many organizations on a city-wide basis to maximize the assistance that can be given to an individual neighborhood.

Each year our society spends some 300 billion dollars through public and private agency's attempts to help the poor. But most of this resource has created dependency among the poor clients and complacency among the workers. The resources are too often directed to contain poverty not to upgrade lives. Instead, the problem is that the system is misconceived and uncoordinated, with the people working at the lowest level having little resources in leadership.

The very systems we have created to help the poor often contribute heavily to the perpetuation of poverty. When two hundred and fifty welfare women are placed together in the same housing project, the disincentives and negative mentality fostered by the welfare structure are reinforced. Their children will all attend the same grade school and the local teacher will have

319

to react to a set of problems for which he has received little training. When the principal calls a PTA meeting, few welfare mothers show up. Thus a valuable forum for change and communication with parents is lost.

As the Church's programs to take help to urban neighborhoods progress, it is essential to organize an intra-city policy committee to attempt to change the entire city's human service delivery system. This body would act as a forum, exchanging ideas on how best to effect institutional change. Leaders from the political, agency, religious, business and community spheres must be involved. The church has the influence sitting in its pews each week to enact changes once it is well-directed.

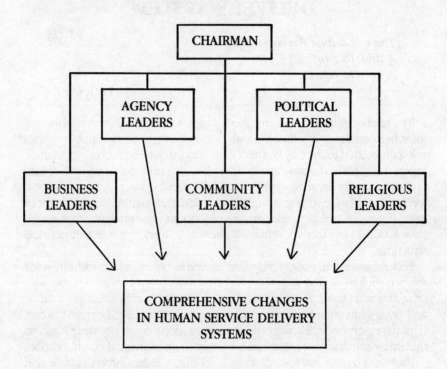

STEP NINETEEN   Organize a city committee.

REVIEW OF THE PROGRAM

REVIEW/PART A
SUMMARY

- SECTION ONE PREMISES
  One Recognize that helping contemporary urban poverty needs different strategies.
  Two Prepare congregations for the complexities of the plan.
  Three Recognize that the "together" people of the urban neighborhood must be involved in all aspects of the program.

- SECTION TWO OBJECTIVES
  One Develop the spiritual effectiveness of the urban church.
  Two Concentrate first on a specific, small, poor neighborhood.
  Three Identify the roles of the Church and the Government.
  Four Have the Church help the Government in their efforts.
  Five Develop effective church programs for the poor.

- SECTION THREE STEPS (OR ACTIVITIES)
  One Find a catalyst in a city who can bring some churches together to help the poor.
  Two Organize four to seven churches.
  Three Select chairmen from each church to form a management committee.
  Four Call a meeting of a cross-section of the congregation to identify individuals interested in serving the poor.
  Five Designate someone from the staff of one of the churches to coordinate the program.
  Six Find an urban church which can be given the staff and resources to effectively serve its neighborhood.
  Seven Develop and survey a specific urban neighborhood around the church.
  Eight Expose members of the congregations to the designated areas.
  Nine Organize the church task forces.
  Ten Form friendship teams to support those people who work with the poor.

Eleven Establish think tanks in the congregations to develop work plans for the neighborhoods.

Twelve Develop skills task forces to apply the skills of the congregation to the needs of the poor.

Thirteen Develop ministry teams to meet the total needs of poor families.

Fourteen Develop a process committee for evaluation and public relations purposes.

Fifteen Train volunteers to manage the program.

Sixteen Develop spiritual ministries in the neighborhood.

Seventeen Develop specific programs in the neighborhood.

Eighteen Replicate results of initial prototype into other poor neighborhoods.

Nineteen Organize a city committee for restructuring the human service delivery system.

REVIEW/PART B
FLOW CHART OF STEPS

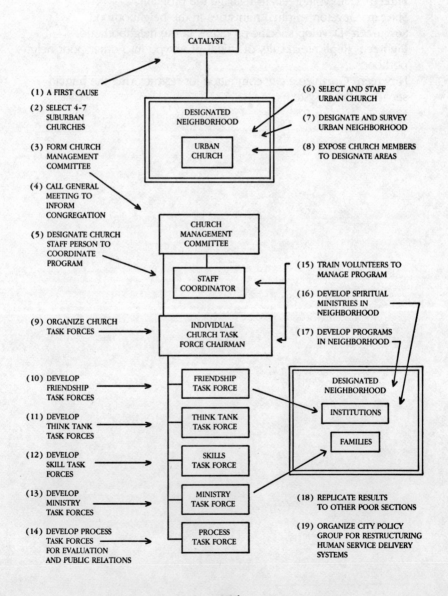

CATALYST

(1) A FIRST CAUSE

(2) SELECT 4-7 SUBURBAN CHURCHES

(3) FORM CHURCH MANAGEMENT COMMITTEE

(4) CALL GENERAL MEETING TO INFORM CONGREGATION

(5) DESIGNATE CHURCH STAFF PERSON TO COORDINATE PROGRAM

(6) SELECT AND STAFF URBAN CHURCH

(7) DESIGNATE AND SURVEY URBAN NEIGHBORHOOD

(8) EXPOSE CHURCH MEMBERS TO DESIGNATE AREAS

DESIGNATED NEIGHBORHOOD

URBAN CHURCH

CHURCH MANAGEMENT COMMITTEE

STAFF COORDINATOR

(15) TRAIN VOLUNTEERS TO MANAGE PROGRAM

(16) DEVELOP SPIRITUAL MINISTRIES IN NEIGHBORHOOD

(17) DEVELOP PROGRAMS IN NEIGHBORHOOD

(9) ORGANIZE CHURCH TASK FORCES

INDIVIDUAL CHURCH TASK FORCE CHAIRMAN

(10) DEVELOP FRIENDSHIP TASK FORCES

FRIENDSHIP TASK FORCE

DESIGNATED NEIGHBORHOOD

INSTITUTIONS

(11) DEVELOP THINK TANK TASK FORCES

THINK TANK TASK FORCE

(12) DEVELOP SKILL TASK FORCES

SKILLS TASK FORCE

FAMILIES

(13) DEVELOP MINISTRY TASK FORCES

MINISTRY TASK FORCE

(18) REPLICATE RESULTS TO OTHER POOR SECTIONS

(14) DEVELOP PROCESS TASK FORCES FOR EVALUATION AND PUBLIC RELATIONS

PROCESS TASK FORCE

(19) ORGANIZE CITY POLICY GROUP FOR RESTRUCTURING HUMAN SERVICE DELIVERY SYSTEMS

REVIEW/PART C

A ROSTER OF POSITIONS NEEDED FOR A CHURCH TO DO THE PROGRAM

Church
Chairman
_____
_____

Friendship Chairman

FRIENDSHIP TEAM MEMBERS

1 _____
2 _____
3 _____
4 _____
5 _____
6 _____
7 _____
8 _____
9 _____
10 _____
11 _____
12 _____

Think Tank Chairman

THINK TANK MEMBERS

Education _____
Recreation/Culture _____
Jobs/Economic Development _____
Housing _____
Drugs _____
Legal/Criminal Justice _____
Medical _____
Welfare/Social Services _____
Spiritual _____
Environmental _____

Skills Chairman

Ministry Chairman

PERSONAL INVENTORY TEAM MEMBERS

Education _____
Social Services _____
Jobs _____
Spiritual _____
Housing _____

MINISTRY COUPLES

1 _____
2 _____
3 _____
4 _____
5 _____

Volunteer Task Force Chairman

Process Chairman _____
Public Relations _____
Evaluation _____

REVIEW/PART D

SOME ORGANIZATIONAL GLUE

. . . If God has given you administrative ability and put you in charge of the work of others, take the responsibility seriously.
                                                            Rom. 12:8

As has been suggested over and over again helping the contemporary urban poor is a complex undertaking. Much coordination is demanded. I would like to pass on some random insights.

1. **The Seminary**   The church's inability to help the poor begins here. It is the function of the seminary to train pastors. Most seminary graduates simply do not know how to minister to the urban poor. Several corrective steps can be made immediately.

   - Develop a definitive poorology and then teach it. If the Bible has so much to say on the subject it merits academic attention.

   - Encourage seminary students to do research projects from church history and biblical studies on the theme of the poor.

   - Outline methodology on how suburban churches can help the poor and teach its membership how to serve more effectively in course work.

   - Develop field work positions and internships in urban and suburban churches which will give practical experience in working with the poor.

   - Launch research efforts into developing great urban ministries much like the medical schools do in their fields. If medical schools have teaching hospitals, why can't seminaries have teaching urban churches?

2. **The Minority Middle Class Churches**   These vital structures must begin to provide more leadership.

   - Make a more concerted effort to lead its laypersons and program emphasis to help the poor.

- Minority middle-class church members must provide exciting and caring role models to the poor.

- They must provide more leadership in the white community to help them to help the poor.

3. **Parachurch Ministries** This has become one of the great phenomena of recent religious development. Huge parachurch ministries like Campus Crusade, Young Life, Youth for Christ, World Vision, Inter-Varsity, and dozens of others have developed and now control vast resources and budgets. The so-called "Electric Church" has developed a whole army of TV ministries. Jerry Falwell, Pat Robertson, Oral Roberts, Bob Schueller, Billy Graham, James Robison and so many others have millions of followers. These parachurch TV ministries represent an unusual new potential resource for the urban church.

- Each parachurch and TV ministry should identify and execute a specific task to help the poor.

- These tasks should be non-competitive

- These tasks should be accomplished through the urban church.

4. **Dialogue with Others** Christians must confer with one another: evangelicals and liberals; denominations and non-denominations; blacks and whites; Christians and Jews. The Hispanic community and the black community—the communication task is endless. But it must begin.

5. **Our Urban Plans Must Lead to Touchdowns** We can't afford to gain a yard with actions because then it will be fourth and seven and we'll have to punt and start all over again. When developing a plan in your city to help the poor, see that it contains the following ingredients. If it doesn't, it might not be able to win.

- **Is it confined in its initial stages to a specific poor neighborhood?** You just can't help everyone at the outset.

- **Is there an emphasis on defining the role of the church and the role of government?** Some claim that before 1935 more than half of all the help to the poor came through the church. Now it is suggested that less than 1% does. But before the church reverses gears once again, it must carefully chart its course.

- **Is there an emphasis on helping legitimate government efforts like schools, police, parks, courts, jails, hospitals, etc?** The church does not have the financial resources or in some cases the authority to duplicate these services. But these institutional structures must be upgraded.

- **Is there a recognition of and strategy that concedes to pluralism in**

American social structures? We live in a nation which guarantees religious freedom to all people. Public institutions are not the arenas of evangelism but of service.

- **Is there evaluation built into all efforts?** It is hard to manage what you can't measure.

- **Is there a planning group (a think tank)?** This research and development arm will be essential for planning. It is also a meaningful vehicle for involving creative people with high creative skills in ministry to the poor.

- **Are there linkages with other cities?** It doesn't make any sense to reinvent wheels. What has worked elsewhere will probably work in your city. Can you find out what is successful elsewhere?

- **Are there some good leaders in your program?** You can't run a program of this nature without some people with good leadership qualities and management experience.

- **Are good, low-cost administrative structures built into the program?** There are available men and women in any community who could and would take over all administrative aspects of the program on a volunteer basis. Helping the poor need not become an expensive pursuit.

- **Does assistance to the poor function on a quid pro quo basis?** Don't give poor people handouts. Make them put something into everything they get.

- **Are people praying for the effort?** We need all the strength, wisdom and love available to accomplish such a difficult task. We must seek God's help.

- **Is there a structure for replication?** Once a prototype neighborhood has been developed, it should be ablt to be replicated elsewhere.

- **Is there a vehicle for restructuring the human service delivery system of a whole city?** Ultimately this must be done but it is a land mine of vested interests.

- **Can the plan be implemented without the extensive use of new monies?** There are few funds available now. Any plan for helping the poor must depend upon skillful restructuring of present resources (using the same people differently) and the infusion of volunteers if it is to remain solvent.

- **Are community people involved in all aspects of planning and implementing change in their neighborhoods?** Without such involvment most efforts will fail.

- **Are minority and white relationships being properly facilitated?** A lot of time can be wasted and improper frustration built into the program if you don't have people who can navigate through potential racial conflicts.

- **Is there a mechanism allowing responsible volunteers to befriend the neighborhood people and identify local needs?** This is where most plans break down. Plans have to be able to filter down to the grass roots.

- **Are there provisions for meeting all the needs of a poor family?** Partial answers usually lead to total failure. We must plan to meet the comprehensive needs of poor families. Meaningful help usually unravels if we don't meet all of a family's needs all at once.

- **Is the urban church structured to meet the needs of the community?** It is very difficult to fit the needs of poor people into middle class institutions. The neighborhood urban church must exist for the needs of its neighborhood and not just for people who drive in on Sunday no matter what their color might be.

6. He planned defensive halfback and was the only sophomore to start on the varsity. In the third game of the season, a series of events happened that greatly affected his future performance. Early in the second quarter, he intercepted a pass. It wasn't a great catch, the ball was thrown at him more than the intended receiver. But in the next series of plays he intercepted another pass—this time in very spectacular fashion. There was a direct relationship between those two catches, the first providing confidence for the second. For the rest of the afternoon, if they had thrown the ball within ten yards of where he was standing, he would have caught it. He believed in himself. The ghetto needs victories. One will come right after another if only a positive pattern can be established. The church can become the catalyst in a great urban renewal.

7. It is essential to maintain momentum. The minister needs to reinforce the good things that are happening. Let people testify to results in the worship service. Put positive happenings in the bulletin. Bring some victory stories to board meetings. The ghetto is shrouded in negative tones. Progress must be reinforced and reinforced and reinforced. Winning is often an attitude. Success is often establishing one.

> *I realize that I really don't even need to mention this to you, about helping God's people. For I know how eager you are to do it. In fact, it was this enthusiasm of yours that stirred up many of them to begin helping.*
>
> II Cor. 9:1, 2

REVIEW/PART E
SOME EXAMPLES

An Example of How A Church Could Be Organized To Help the Poor

Dr. George Smith of the First Christian Church went to lunch with a good pastor friend of his who impressed him with the need to help the poor. Because of the government budget cuts Dr. Smith had been thinking for some time that his church had to do more in this area. But he just didn't know what to do. The lunch with his friend helped to clarify some things.

Dr. Smith attended a meeting with four other pastors and the five of them decided to join together to help the poor. One of the five represented a large black church with over two thousand members. The five pastors met once a week for six weeks to plan their strategy.

They invited a small black church in a very poor section of town to join their efforts. The neighborhood around the urban church was chosen as the target area. Each church selected a chairman and they were to comprise a management committee to run the project.

Dr. Smith identified six potential candidates from his church for the position of chairman. Each was qualified. He had dinner with them all and carefully watched their responses. While all were enthusiastic and supportive Cris Pond clearly had the best insights. Later that evening Dr. Smith asked him to become the chairman and he readily accepted.

Dr. Smith then went to an assistant minister on his staff named Charles Andrews. Charlie was head of adult ministries and community programs. He asked Charlie to take responsibility for working closely with Cris Pond on this project.

Cris Pond joined the chairmen from the other churches and they created a management committee to give leadership to the program. Charles Andrews also attended all the meetings as did clergy representatives from the other churches.

Dr. Smith, Cris Pond and Rev. Andrews met and decided to invite about 100 members of the congregation to come to a meeting about the poor. They also invited the pastor from the church in the poor neighborhood to address the crowd. The Sunday before the meeting, Dr. Smith had spoken about the parable of the Good Samaritan. The meeting was a great success. Nearly all of the hundred who attended volunteered to help.

Dr. Smith, Cris Pond and Rev. Andrews then held another meeting. They selected five persons to head up their task forces. Joe Becker, a senior vice-president of an insurance company was selected to head up the friendship task force. Sally Rand, the head librarian at the city library was asked to become head of the think tank. Sam Cummings, a foreman at the phone company was chosen to lead the skills task force. Grace Peters, a dedicated principal of a grade school and an effective teacher of the adult Sunday school class was asked to head up the ministry committee. Henry Matthews, a Professor of Management at the University Business School was chosen to head up the process committee. All agreed to serve. Three weeks later Dr. Smith preached another sermon on the poor and publicly introduced the plan and the chairpersons to the congregation.

Sally Rand, chairperson of the think tank, selected ten members of the congregation to join her think tank. Most of those chosen came from the members who had volunteered at the meeting several weeks before.

These people from the parish had expertise in areas of education, recreational and cultural activities, housing, jobs, social services, drug and alcohol abuse, criminal justice systems, medical, spiritual and environmental. They joined members from other congregations to form a matrixed think tank (the educators from the churches met together, the social services people, etc.)

Joe Becker, chairman of the friendship task force, selected five members of the church to join his committee. These were also folks who had been to the earlier meeting. These five members joined representatives from the other churches to form five task forces with one person from each church. The task forces went to meet with the principal of a grade school, the head of a housing project, the leader of a Boy's Club, a police sergeant and head of a welfare unit. They offered their friendship and help and asked each to come up with problems and day dreams. They were enthusiastically welcomed and soon received their lists. The lists from the friendship committees were given to the think tanks and soon ideas and insights were translated into solutions. Now it was Sam Cummings, chairman of the skills committee's turn. He took the plans of the think tanks and gave them to members of the congregation who had the skills to implement them. Within weeks the skills of the parish were being given to meet the needs of the institutions.

Meanwhile, the think tanks were not only responding to the requests of the institutional leaders but were also creating comprehensive solutions in each of their program areas. Within several months they had figured out how individual families could get most of their needs met either through revamped institutions' resources or through programs initiated by the church. These plans were given to skill task forces for implementation.

Grace Peters, chairperson of the ministry task force, had been hard at work for several months. She had recruited and helped train a personal inventory team. It consisted of a social worker, an educator, a jobs person, a financial planner and a spiritual leader from the congregation. These were highly motivated and gifted members who had agreed to spend one evening a week for the next year analyzing the comprehensive needs of a family. Grace was also training couples from the parish who had volunteered to help implement the prescriptions of help which would be drawn up by the personal inventory teams. There was great excitement in the congregations as the first personal inventory and ministry teams went to meet with the first family. By the end of the first year the church had couples from the church helping 37 poor families including over 200 individuals. There were some amazing success stories.

Sandra Becker, wife of the chairman of the friendship committee, was selected to head up the Dorcas program. These were persons of the church who had volunteered to help to administer all aspects of the program.

Meanwhile, Henry Matthews had developed his process committee. He had asked a successful young advertising executive to head up his public relations efforts. The ad man was conducting tours of the ghetto, producing bulletin inserts, circulating a newsletter he had developed and had attractive posters all over the church. Henry himself had developed the beginning of a comprehensive Management Information system charting all progress.

In November, seven months after the program had begun, Dr. Smith dedicated a Sunday morning service to a comprehensive review of the program. A poor family shared the miracle of their new lives with the congregation. The congregation was very moved. Dr. Smith preached a powerful sermon and challenged the parish to produce more volunteers. Over 500 responded to the invitation for service. The choir sang a closing song with deep emotion. A new spirit was beginning to spread through the church. Dr. Smith pronounced the benediction in a voice of thanksgiving.

An Example of a Chairman's Meeting in Action
The program was composed of six churches. The First Baptist Church had 8,000 members and was the largest church in town. The First Christian Church had 4,000 members. The Cresent Avenue Missionary Baptist Church was a black congregation with 2,000 members. The Grace Bible Church had 1,500 members. The Our Savior Lutheran Church had 500 members. The Mt. Zion Baptist Church had 100 members and was located in a very poor section of town. The project consisted of a twenty block area around that church, including a housing project.

Each church had a chairman. Robert Johnson from the First Baptist Church was the overall chairman. They met at 7:30 every other Wednesday morning. In addition to the chairmen, all of whom were laymen, clergymen came from each church. Women, representing each church, also came to carry out administrative functions. The following are minutes from a meeting:

AGENDA ITEM ONE   Approval of Think Tank Projects for Skills Committee Implementation

John Cleveland chairman of the church think tanks gave a report on the three programs that had been approved.

1. The grade school principal wanted to start a school band program and the think tank was convinced there were enough instruments lying around in attics of the combined congregations to outfit ten bands.

2. Many of the window screens in the housing project were ripped and the city had no money to replace them. The think tanks took the measurements and were convinced that there were enough screens in enough church members' garages to meet a crucial need.

3. There were many vacant lots in the neighborhood which were eyesores. The think tank wanted to launch "project dirt." Each congregation on a designated Saturday would move as much dirt as they could collect into the neighborhood.

All three programs were approved by the committee. The skills committee of First Baptist was given the task of coordinating the musical instrument project, Cresent Avenue the screen project, and Our Savior the dirt project.

AGENDA ITEM TWO   Approval of a New Friendship Committee for Recreational Center in the Housing Project

Pete Rutherford of Grace Bible, chairman of its friendship task force asked that the committee approve a new friendship task force for the recreational center in the housing project. Sam Jones heads it up and he has no staff working for him. He has responsibility for over 600 children and is completely inundated with the needs of his program. The management committee agreed to set up its sixth friendship committee.

AGENDA ITEM THREE   The Creation of a Manual for the Ministry Teams

After seven months there were now over 250 families involved with ministry teams from the congregations. Grace Peters, chairperson from the ministry task force of the Christian Church, felt that the program should draw up a manual to help new members with their responsibility. By now there was enough experience so that many successful principles could be documented. The management committee agreed that a skills task force should be designated to develop the manual and that they work in close collaboration with the process task force's evaluation unit.

AGENDA ITEM FOUR   Funding for the Staffing of the Urban Church

Three new staff persons were needed for the urban church. Dr. George Smith from the Christian Church recommended that a Christmas collection be taken up in each of the churches to fund the salaries. This would entail sacrifices on the part of the more affluent. The management committee accepted the idea subject to individual church approval, set a goal of $38,000 and asked the public relations people of the process task force to produce materials by December 18th.

AGENDA ITEM FIVE   Changing the Vocational Tests

Some serious dissension exists among the personal inventory teams about which vocational tests to use. Bad feelings have arisen and must be resolved. Sandra Becker wondered if threatening to cut them in half would force the babies to stop fighting. The chairman thanked her for playing Solomon but felt that the issue should be dealt with immediately. Chairman Johnson asked for someone to volunteer to be peacemaker. No one offered. Chairman Johnson asked Sandra Becker to use her acknowledged charm to resolve the disputes. She agreed and will make recommendations to the committee at the next meeting.

REVIEW/PART F

DEVELOP TIME FRAMES FOR VOLUNTEER ACTIVITY

Appoint judges and administrative officials for all the cities the Lord your God is giving you. They will administer justice in every part of the land. . . . Justice must prevail.

Deut. 16:18-20

Time is a valuable possession. If people volunteer to help the poor, their activities must be carefully managed. A good plan for a congregation is to have great diversity and flexibility. Not everybody has the same availability. The following list gives some examples of monthly time spent helping the poor.

Mr. James Smith	68	Retired	Spends ten hours a week playing chess with urban students in the school cafeteria. He has become an unofficial counsellor to many sharing a lifetime of wisdom with some urban need.
Ms. Jenny Aken	52	Librarian	Spends four hours a week helping members of a wealthy parish give the right kinds of books to an urban high school whose fund for new book purchases has been virtually eliminated.
Carolyn Brown	16	Student	Tutors an eight year old girl from an urban school two hours a week. The little girl is far behind in reading skills.

Mr. Pete Vanderbush	42	Factory Worker	Helped to organize and coach a little league baseball team in the ghetto. Spends around ten hours a week during a three month season.
Mrs. Ellen Craft	32	Housewife	Goes into the poor section of town and takes a welfare mother shopping for food with her once a week. Time for extra travel—one hour.
Mr. Ralph Baker	48	Computer Manager	Runs a seminar of six urban sixth graders once a month on a Saturday morning. Time commitment—four hours a month.
Mrs. Sally Conners	29	Housewife	Volunteers four hours a week to work in an urban day care center. Brings her own two children along.
Mrs. Bona Day	68	Senior Citizen	Visits an urban hospital three hours a week.
Mr. Tom Craft	56	C.P.A.	Helps an urban church two hours a month with the financial records.
George Clark	20	College Student	Has developed independent study projects with two urban ninth grade boys. Spends three hours a week one night a week with his students.

REVIEW/PART G

ATTEMPT TO OVERCOME INEVITABLE NEGATIVE REACTION

Oh, come back to God. Live by the principles of love and justice and always be expecting much from him, your God.

Hos. 12:6

It must be considered that there is nothing more difficult to carry out, nor more doubtful of success, nor more dangerous to handle, than to initiate a new order of things. For the reformer has enemies in all those who profit by the old order, and only lukewarm defenders in all those who would profit by the new.

Machavelli

The Prince

Because of the hectic pace and demands of the summer program, every bit of space was used in the church including the sanctuary. The sanctuary became an all-purpose room, offering a place to assemble, to take a nap on a pew, or to hold a small meeting in a deserted corner.

A church leader came into the sanctuary and asked to see me. I was running a meeting with some of the fellows behind the church pulpit. I left the meeting and walked over to the elder. He was facing the pulpit and my back was to it. As we conversed, I could see that the elder was becoming more and more distracted by something taking place behind me.

One of the fellows I had been meeting with, Raymond Cook, was a very big man. He had an exceptionally large posterior. After I had left the meeting, the fellows had spontaneously called a recess until I returned. Raymond got up to stretch and then decided to sit down. He sat on the pulpit. His posterior completely covered it with lots left over.

I can't remember what the man talked to me about. It was probably some extension of the elder's authority in the service of his church—like the wine bottles found in the bathroom, or a broken chair in the prayer hall, or some profanity scribbled on the hall wall.

Well, suddenly the elder could no longer believe his eyes. Protruding from the pulpit was Raymond's posterior. We would have to go way back into the Old Testament to the episode of Balaam before we encountered a man of God so disturbed by a posterior. The elder finally exploded. "Nigger get your posterior off of our pulpit." The scene became real emotional.

Now Raymond shouldn't have been sitting there and the elder was right in asking him to get off. But I wondered, "What if the elder could get up the same emotional response towards the cries of the ghetto—all the needy posteriors sitting on all the stoops on the streets of Harlem."

One time the Master said, "You pay tithes of mint and dill and cummin; but you have overlooked the weightier demands of the law, justice, mercy, and good faith. You strain at a gnat but swallow a camel!"

Attempting to implement a plan as complex as this will inevitably incur negative reactions. When you suggest a new way of doing something, folks who have been traditionally responsible will feel defensive. There will be people with legitimate reasons for suggesting different approaches. There will be other folks who have emotional needs to be negative. Old personality conflicts will sometimes be brought into the development of new ideas. Theological differences are a fact of life and some might not be able to be resolved. Race issues which have divided America for decades and decades could be raised anew with a vengeance. No one should delude himself that a new imaginative plan will not threaten established interests. Nor should anyone believe that the plan will conciliate age-old antagonists.

From long years of conflict experience, I would make four recommendations:

1. **Strive for communication.** These are difficult plans to implement because they go against so many existing structures, content areas, and issues. People need time to understand. Let us take time; as much as is reasonably needed. Don't allow folks to follow a plan which has been imposed on them. Rather let them understand and become excited.

2. **Make the effort well managed.** If you don't, people who had doubts or negative tendencies to begin with will attempt to attack the efforts not on the worth of the plan but on some administrative malfunction.

3. **Resolve conflicts.** Don't allow either personality conflicts or conceptual ones to escalate into issues that could destroy the whole program. Not everyone will want to go with the plan and some will have good reasons. But conflicts must be resolved with skill and compassion.

4. **Keep the program spiritually directed.** This is the only real help for the poor, the only thing that can motivate the volunteers and the only thing that will keep divisions to a minimum.

338

REVIEW/PART H
REAL LOVE HAS A PLAN

neighborhoods die
one block at a time

that's the only way
they will be resurrected

no decay
is irreversible
what is needed
is a force
and a plan

God has the force
in the people who love Him
what is needed
is a plan

real love
has a plan
the deeper the love
the greater the plan

arise oh people of God
and be about the plan
we must reorganize
our whole structures
that serve the poor
get the unions
get the politicians
bring the minority middle class
get the corporations
get the people of the ghetto
get the universities

get the churches
get the synogogues
get everybody working together
meeting
planning
reorganizing
and then tell everyone
about our Lord
and the people
the together people of the ghetto
those who work so hard for so little
and the beaten people of the ghetto
and those in drugs and wine and nothing
many will respond
to the talk of the people of God
because it has been expressed
in good works

"faith that doesn't show itself
by good works
is no faith at all
it is dead and useless . . ."

EPILOGUE

words have their limitations
even the best
fall short

but words have a time
those open periods of history
when events force the need for answers

the time of the ghetto has come again
budget cuts and the needs of the poor
have created the necessity for the new
such moments are either seized
or lost

if all the people
who wanted to help the poor
and all the poor
who wanted help
could only exchange their desires
the ghettos of America would be changed
that great dream
will only happen
if words produce a meaningful plan
and that strategy is implemented

this particular plan
was born in action
and molded by failure
and inspired by the Scriptures
but it is written on paper
not stone
if you want to refine it
or change it
or help implement it
please write to me

The value of a plan lies not in its appearance on paper but in its effective application. The strategy depicted in this book is not theoretical; it is a description of what is now happening in Dallas, Texas and in other cities in America with the coordinating assistance of the STEP Foundation.

Harv Oostdyk
Post Office Box 528
Manhattanville Station
New York, New York 10027